Praise for 7 Ideas

"Revolutionary."

"I am excited to see this book used through missionary efforts to inform and ignite people around the world."

"First and foremost I would like to thank you for writing this amazing book."

"7 Ideas that Changed the World serves as a treetop introduction for the greatest ideas of human history, all of which come from the Bible."

"Mitchell's bold thesis is eloquently stated, well-supported, and infinitely important."

"I think this this book clearly and effectively explains how Christianity has impacted our world. Even as a Christian myself, I was surprised by how much our faith has influenced our culture."

"7 Ideas That Changed the World was incredible. I absolutely enjoyed reading this book. This book opened my eyes up to ideas that I had never even thought of before."

"Christianity is the single most influential thing to ever happen to the shaping of Western Culture."

"7 Ideas That Changed the World is a book that everyone needs to read right now."

"It is amazing how the changing of a person through the gospel changes entire communities, cultures, and then societies as a whole."

"I loved this book!"

"Thank you so much for writing a book that has meaning and power."

"The 7 Ideas that Changed the World is a literary treasure to those who need to see the goodness of Christianity in the world."

7 Ideas That
Changed the World

Discover How the Bible Builds
and Transforms Civilizations

Learn How Biblical Truths
Shape the World You Live In.

Dr. Philip Mitchell

First Edition

v1.1.2020

First Printing, 2020

ISBN 978-1-7342390-0-3

Published by:
Micaiah Ministries
c/o Philip Mitchell
10149 W. 55th Drive #206
Arvada, CO 80002
pmitchell@ccu.edu

Table of Contents

Dedicated to my loving wife and family,
all the missionaries with whom I have served,
and all the people God has blessed through our work.

Introduction

My Story

I am a college professor and a pastor. I grew up in a small town in Wyoming where I went to church every Sunday. My Christian community taught me the value of the Bible and its power to change my life, but my religious background contained no interest in the wider culture around me. Like most small-town American Christians, we focused on our own little world and left everywhere else to its own devices.

In 1969 I began my pastoral ministry. Since then I have never stopped preaching or teaching the Bible in the church. I love and defend the inerrant Word of God, and witness on a daily basis the power of the Scripture working in people's lives, guiding them to God's life and salvation.

On August 16, 1975, I married the love of my life, Nancy. We have since raised nine children together, three of whom we adopted. Our dedication of such a large portion of our lives to our diverse children is one way we live out our faith.

Several years after my marriage, my life took a turn. I left my pastoral role at a church in California and followed God's call into a university. I received my Ph.D. in History in 1992 and began my 25 years of lecturing at the University of Colorado as a professor of history.

However, my days as a pastor were not over. In 1990 some fellow believers and I planted a church in Niwot, Colorado. My life was full of children, teaching history, and preaching the Word. But God, as always, had more to teach me.

In 1999, I left the North American continent for the first time. I went to visit several members of my church in the Southeast Asian country of Cambodia. These fellow Christians, inspired by their faith, had moved to Cambodia to start orphanages and schools. I, of all people, though I hated to fly and seldom left home, became the leader of their organization. My visit was pastoral as well as personal. As soon as I got off the plane, I knew things were different. Very different. It wasn't just the heat, the smells, the traffic, or the poverty—it was the culture. The culture of Cambodia was alien to the Western Christian culture I had grown up in, and for the first time in my life I personally experienced the depth of this truth: Culture impacts everything.

When I returned from Cambodia, I began to study more: What exactly makes culture so powerful? The scholar Christopher Dawson writes, "Culture is the name which has been given to man's social inheritance—to all that men have learnt from the past by the process of imitation, education and learning and to all that they hand on in like manner to their descendants and successors."[1] A culture is basically the social climate of a place. Allow me to give an illustration:

I live in Colorado, in the middle of North America, and more than a thousand miles from the nearest ocean. In the winter, Colorado gets very cold and snowy, so I, like many other old people, like to fly to the West Coast of my country. When I get off the plane I am in an entirely different world. Instead of snow and ice, I see palm trees and lush vegetation. The temperature never gets below freezing. Many beautiful flowers are in bloom, whereas around my home all is silent and dormant. A person knowledgeable in weather and climate would tell you that the difference is the nearness of the ocean. This massive body of water completely changes the climate, but the people on the West Coast do not get up every morning and say, "Thank you, God, for the ocean! Without the ocean we would all be freezing cold." No, they do not give the ocean a minute's thought. They simply enjoy the climate. The ocean is the whole reason for their climate, but the fact seldom occurs to them. So it is with Christian culture. The social, political, and philosophical impacts of Christianity affect everything in our lives in a wonderful, positive way, but we never think about the source of these benefits, or give glory to the Lord, who gave it to us. However, if we trace the roots of these blessings, we can see the Lord's hand at work throughout history.

In my classes at the University of Colorado in Boulder, I lectured mainly on the history of Western civilization. My studies showed me that the great movements of philosophy, the enlightenment, the roots of science, the inspiration for every movement of human rights—so much of what we Westerners take for granted—stem from Western culture. When I returned from Cambodia, I began to emphasize the origins of culture. Why had Western culture specifically become the most powerful in the history of the world? Why was it influential everywhere on earth? In my research, I discovered that what made Western culture different was its ideas, and every single idea came from the Bible, the most influential book of all time. My passions for history and scripture became one.

Journalist David Aikman asked the same question and discovered a sim-

---

[1] Dawson, Christopher. *The Formation of Christendom*. Sheed and Ward, 1967. p.39

ilar answer. He spoke to a Chinese scholar who had spent a great deal of time trying to answer the same question: why is Western culture so powerful? Why is it successful and preeminent all over the world? According to this scholar, "We studied everything we could from the historical, political, economic, and cultural perspective. ... We have realized that the heart of your culture is your religion: Christianity. That is why the West has been so powerful. ... We have no doubt about this." [2]

This Chinese scholar recognized something many Western scholars are blind to. In fact, many modern historians ignore or misrepresent the role of the Christian faith in the formation of our culture. However, according to my own lifetime of study and experience, as well as the findings of many experts in Western Civilization: Western culture is overwhelmingly the product of Christian thinking. Without Christianity, Western culture would not exist.

A major problem in Western culture today is the assumption of Christian values without admitting they are Christian. For example, many in the West assume the equality of women is innate—a natural idea that needs only to be excavated from the ground of truth. But the ideas of equality, human rights, and even human worth are only "natural" in Christian culture. One of the tasks we have as Christians is helping people realize where their "innate" values actually come from. Most studies are all about looking ahead. Science, business, politics, the arts—all these are about progress and innovation. History, on the other hand, helpfully traces ideas backward through time, right to their source. The study of history traces the modern idea of women's rights to the ancient ideas of Christianity.

As I began to speak to my students about these world-shaping ideas, I compiled a long list of reasons that Western culture has become the powerful influence it is today. I connected specific ideas that shaped Western civilization with their origins in the Bible. These uniquely Biblical ideas are the primary elements of a healthy culture.

Let me be clear about what I have found: all humans are equally valuable, but not all cultures are equally valuable. A mistake many Westerners make is to equate culture with ethnicity. The seven ideas of this book are for all ethnicities, but they stand in opposition to many cultures. All cultures contain admirable elements, but not all cultures are healthy climates in which a society can thrive. In order for society to progress, some cultural aspects must be eliminated and

---

[2] Aikman, David. *Jesus in Beijing: How Christianity Is Transforming China and Changing the Global Balance of Power.* Monarch, 2006. p.5

replaced. Other cultural aspects are kept, incorporated, and even furthered because of Christianity. For example, early Christians took on Greek ideas that were compatible with Christian doctrine. They borrowed the Greek scholarly process to study their own doctrine. Christianity has never hesitated to appreciate and incorporate those aspects of a culture they thought were consistent with Christianity's core beliefs.

In addition, Christian theology clearly teaches that other religions and cultures contain truth. Christians expect to find truth in other cultures on the basis of General Revelation—the belief that God has revealed truth to everyone through the natural world (Romans 1: 19, 20). For example, a number of years ago a British philosopher named David Conway published a list of the attributes of God as taught by Aristotle. The list was remarkably similar to that taught in the Bible, even though Aristotle never had access to any biblical writings. He gained insights into the nature of God just by observing the natural world.

Finally, not all these characteristics occur evenly in all Christian cultures, but they all appear in varying degree. And though these characteristics do appear sporadically in non-Christian culture, they cannot be sustained without the guidance of Christianity and the Bible.

In 2015 I visited northern Thailand, where I lectured to a staff of Thai tribesmen on the influence of the Bible in the world. At the completion of my lecture, one tribal elder stood and gave a passionate response. Since he was speaking in his native tongue, I did not understand a word he said but I could sense his emotion. After he sat down, my translator turned to me and said, "This gentleman wants everyone to know how thankful he is that God has revealed these truths in the Bible and how thankful he is that they have come to his people." The translator then went on to say that this tribe had struggled with feelings of inferiority, but now they possessed the most powerful ideas in the history of the world. These ideas filled them with confidence and hope.

I want to share these seven ideas with more people. I want to communicate my lifetime spent witnessing the power of the Bible in culture. I want you, my reader, to be filled with the same confidence and hope that inspired my Thai brothers and sisters.

This book is about the most powerful ideas that have ever entered the human mind. These ideas have shaped the destiny of the human race more than any other influence. They have more power to change your life than any philosophy you have ever heard. I pray they will move your heart and mind the way they have moved the world.

A Brief History of Christian Culture

Is this book about Christian culture or Western culture? Well, both: The ideas are all Biblical, but the history is mostly Western.

However, it all began in the East. Four thousand years ago, God chose to descend to earth and communicate His truth to human beings. He started with one particular man—Abraham. In Genesis 12:1 the Bible says, "And God spoke to Abraham ..." It was one of the single most important moments of all time. Abraham's faith spread from a personal faith to a family faith. When God spoke He communicated unique truths about Himself to Abraham's descendants, particularly those of his grandson Jacob, who was renamed by God: Israel. This one man had so many descendants that his faith spread from a family faith to a national faith: the faith of Judaism. Over the next thousand years, Jews began to record the part of scripture that Christians today call the Old Testament. Moses, David, Solomon, the prophets, and several others recorded the history, wisdom, and warnings of God during the generations that followed.

Next, God chose to become a human being in the Jewish man Jesus Christ and step up His revelatory action in a dramatic way. In the generations after Jesus, the followers of Jesus have spread these unique truths about God to the far corners of the earth. They not only preached, but wrote down eyewitness accounts of Jesus' life and teachings. They carefully compiled these writings into what we know as the New Testament today.

Since its origin, the Biblical record has been preserved more carefully than any other document in history. No other ancient document has been preserved, copied, and translated with more care. However, if God had not spoken, no one would know or believe these ideas today. The Bible is the direct revelation of God himself.

After the life of Christ, God used Western culture to spread the influence of Christianity across Europe. The national faith of the Jews has, through Christianity, become an international faith. Christianity and Christians themselves have since formed the basis for the most influential and powerful forces in history, particularly in Great Britain and the United States.

More recently, Christianity is coming back to the East. Though Western culture contains the history of these ideas, Christianity and the Bible contain the ideas themselves. As Christian missionaries continue to preach throughout the world, the faith of the West is becoming the faith known to all. As Revelation predicts, those "from every nation, from all tribes and peoples and languages" will one day believe (Revelation 7:9). Praise God!

The 7 Ideas That Changed the World:

1. The Sanctity of Life

2. The Value of Women

3. Ministries of Compassion

4. Social Justice

5. Free Will

6. Sexual Ethics

7. Christian Roots of Science & Technology

CHAPTER 1
The Sanctity of Life

○━━━━━━━━━━━━━━━━━○

So God created man in his own image,
in the image of God he created him—Genesis 1:27

Sanctity: Ultimate importance and inviolability. (Oxford English Dictionary)

Are all people equally valuable, or are some people more valuable than others? To most people in Western culture, this is an offensive question. However, many cultures assume that some people are more important than others: the rich, the successful, the powerful. These cultures also assume that some people are less valuable than others: the weak, the sick, the poor, and those with special needs. If a culture bases worth and value on ability or family status, then those less useful or low-born are less valuable. If a culture bases worth on power, than those who are weaker are less valuable. The source of human worth is at the center of culture.

My daughter was in the hospital with her infant, special-needs son. He was near death because his lungs were underdeveloped and he caught pneumonia easily. When the attending doctor found out that my daughter was adopting this little boy, he grew hostile. "Why would you adopt someone like this?" he asked, "Spend your time and money on a healthy child." The doctor said this because he did not know or believe the Bible's teaching that this little boy is as important to God as the richest man in the world. Christian culture bases worth, not on utility or power, but on our equal value before God.

The Biblical Basis for the Sanctity of Life

Genesis 1 contains the most powerful statement about life ever made in human history: "So God created man in his own image, **in the image of God** he created him; male and female he created them" (Genesis 1:27, emphasis added). No one sentence has affected life on this planet like this one.

This verse tells your story: Before the universe was created, you existed only in the mind of God. God knew you when no one else did. Ephesians 1:4 states plainly that God "chose us in him before the creation of the world to be holy and blameless in his sight." He has always known you the best and loved you the most. You have infinite worth and value to Him. You are precious in the eyes of God. Each human is uniquely created and uniquely loved by their creator God. In Psalm 139:15, 16 the writer proclaims the kind of worth he knows he has as God's beloved creation, "For you created my inmost being. You knit me together in my mother's womb. I praise you, for I am fearfully and wonderfully made."

Consider the implications of this truth: God loves every man, woman, and child. Equally. Totally. God did not say that some men are created in His image and some are not. He does not discriminate based on age, race, gender, social status, or any other characteristic. Galatians 3:28 makes this abundantly clear: "There is neither Jew nor Gentile, neither slave nor free, nor is there male and female, for you are all one in Christ Jesus."

All mankind has infinite worth and value in the eyes of God. The powerful man who rules over a nation has infinite worth and value in the eyes of God, but no more than the humble beggar who lives outside the palace. The rich and wealthy are valuable to God, and so are the poor and suffering. An unborn baby is infinitely valuable, and so is an elderly woman with severe Alzheimer's disease. The intelligent are valuable to God, and so are the mentally retarded. The weak and sick are of infinite worth and value, as are the blind, the deaf, and those who cannot walk.

How can this be? People are made in God's image. People are more like God than any other being in the universe. We have abilities that do not exist in animals. Only people create art, speak languages, and make moral decisions— good and bad. One author observed, "It is not as though men do art well and dogs do art poorly. Dogs don't do art at all." Even animals such as elephants who "paint" were taught to do so by people. Not only do we have dominion over the animals, but the Bible teaches that one day we will rule over the angels (I Corinthians 6:3). You will organize heavenly hosts. That is how special you are. You are more than an accident, and more than an animal. You are infinitely loved, infinitely valuable, and infinitely chosen by God. This is the Christian basis for the sanctity of life.

How Does the Sanctity of Life Impact Culture?

Cultures believe either that all people are valuable, or that only some people are valuable. In my own country, the United States of America, we do not realize the basis of our belief that all people are created equal. The citizens of Western culture have been given a glorious sense of worth and purpose, but we think we created it ourselves. Instead of believing that we are created by God, more and more people in my culture are beginning to believe that we are formed by evolution. The problem is that evolution does not promise equal worth to all humans. The idea that humans are valuable is a gift of Christian culture, not our genetic code. It was God Himself who insisted on the inherent worth of all human beings. Ironically, I have yet to meet an atheistic college professor who did not accept that all humans are valuable, but none will accept that the source of this value is God. They assume that all cultures value human life the way we do, but not all cultures do.

The Sanctity of Life in Non-Christian Cultures

Most cultures do not believe in the sanctity of life. Without this foundational belief, people (usually the rich and powerful) draw lines to distinguish who is more valuable, and who is less. In the ancient world, some people were considered to have little to no value, depending on their social status.

Children and old people, physically the weakest members of society, are usually the ones whose value is questioned first. Many cultures have developed acceptable ways to get rid of unwanted children. In her book, *May You Be the Mother of a Hundred Sons*, Elisabeth Bumiller writes that poisoning unwanted children is a common practice in India.[3] Children, even though they are the future, have been abused and devalued in many cultures. The same is true for the elderly. Euthanasia has been routinely practiced in many cultures. Without the protection of the sanctity of life, the weak become prey to the strong.

One great evidence of the devaluing of human life throughout history is in human sacrifice. In these cultures, the less valuable members of society were literally sacrificed. This was a common practice in the ancient world. The Middle Eastern Canaanites would offer up their children to their gods. Jeremiah called this "making your children pass through the fire" (Jeremiah 19:5).

Human sacrifice was a large part of ancient Aztec culture. I have stood in the great anthropological museum in Mexico City. Inside a platform that sat on top of ancient pyramids is a sluice way to siphon off the large amounts of blood produced in religious ceremonies. The museum has sculptures of children crying because they are about to be sacrificed. Real children endured this by the thousands. In a period of several generations, the Aztecs sacrificed two

---

[3] Elizabeth Bumiller, *May You Be the Mother of a Hundred Sons* (London: Penguin, 1998)

million victims to their gods.[4] On special feast days, they would sacrifice tens of thousands, including many children. The tribes of northern Europe would also routinely sacrifice children to "harvest gods" to ensure a good crop. After victory in battle, they would sacrifice captured victims and then eat them.

The Carthaginians of North Africa practiced child sacrifice. The infant Hannibal had been selected. However, his father secretly substituted a slave boy in his stead, and Hannibal was spared. Before Hannibal became one of the greatest military leaders of all time, his life was considered worthless. His culture did not recognize the sanctity of life.[5]

But human sacrifice was not limited to children. When a Viking chieftain died, many young women would be sacrificed and burned with him in order to accompany him into the afterlife. This culture believed that the powerful chieftain was more valuable than the young women sacrificed in his honor.

Ancient Greece and Rome are prime examples of cultures that did not believe in the sanctity of life. The great Greek philosopher Aristotle said that nature teaches us that some men are inferior to other men, and that all women are inferior to men. He argued that this is a logical deduction from looking at the natural world. Aristotle's kind of discrimination was rampant in Greek culture. The ancient Greeks regularly practiced abortion even though the Hippocratic oath forbids it. Plato argued that it was the prerogative of the state to force a woman to have an abortion, so the state would not become too populated. Sadly, children had little value even after birth. Unwanted children were commonly disposed of like trash. They were taken from their homes and exposed to the elements until they died. The great Roman philosopher and orator Cicero believed that deformed infants should be killed.[6] Suicide was also common, even encouraged, in ancient Greece and Rome. Without a basis for self-worth, people became violent toward themselves. Greece and Rome were cultures of death.

These examples of abortion, infanticide, discrimination, and suicide are making a comeback in modern, Western culture. Richard Dawkins, a professor

---

[4] "History of the Conquest of Mexico by William H. Prescott." *Goodreads,* Goodreads, 4 Dec. 2001, www.goodreads.com/book/show/901365.History_of_the_Conquest_of_Mexico.

[5] Lamb, Harold. "Hannibal: One Man Against Rome." *Amazon,* Amazon, 1 Jan. 1970, www.amazon.com/Hannibal-One-Man-Against-Rome/dp/B0006AVNS2.

[6] Cicero (106–43 B.C.) justified infanticide, at least for the deformed, by citing the ancient Twelve Tables of Roman law when he says that "deformed infants shall be killed" Alvin J. Schmidt, *How Christianity Changed the World* (Kindle Locations 945-946). Zondervan. Kindle Edition.

at Oxford, told a pregnant woman that instead of having a child with some birth defects she should abort it and try for a better child.[7] Iceland has recently been in the news for trying to eliminate Down syndrome by aborting every baby in whom it is detected.[8] This is obvious discrimination against individuals with special needs—individuals of equal worth to every other human according to God. Peter Singer, a professor (ironically) of ethics, argued that parents should have the right to abort a child up to the age of two![9] This hatred of human life has sent tremors through the self-worth of even our most lauded celebrities. Robin Williams, Marilyn Monroe, and Chester Bennington all famously took their own lives in the last century. Devaluing life impacts everyone in the surrounding culture.

Without a basis for the sanctity of life, some cultures breed death.

The Sanctity of Life in Christian Culture

The United States' Declaration of Independence states that "all men are created equal." This is something every U.S. citizen takes for granted, but equality has no philosophical basis without the belief in the sanctity of life.

In ancient Rome, gladiatorial contests were as popular as soccer is today. Thousands of spectators attended these events, with no regard for the lives being snuffed out in front of them. The early Christians condemned those spectacles and drew criticism from the Roman intelligentsia. However, Christian culture made enough headway that, within 400 years, the contests were abolished. Western intellectuals today view the Roman circuses with horror. Why did their academic counterparts in Rome have the opposite reaction? The difference is Christian culture.

Christian culture values life the way God values it—from conception onward. This is why Christian culture opposes abortion. The more a nation is under the influence of Christian culture, the more it opposes the ending of life in the womb. The United States is now considered post-Christian, which is why abortion is legal. Even our cultural elite now favor abortion on demand. However, I have noticed that their defense of this barbaric practice almost always includes defining the unborn as non-human. Supreme Court Justice Harry Blackmun in his dreadful Roe v. Wade majority opinion referred many times to the unborn as "potentially human." In order for Justice Blackmun to countenance abortion, he had to define the unborn down to a subhuman level. This is

---

[7] *The Guardian,* August 21, 2014;
[8] Patricia Heaton, *America,* December 4, 2017
[9] Nat Hentoff, Washington Post, September 11, 1999

a backhanded acknowledgment of the sanctity of life.

Every year my church remembers the Supreme Court decision legalizing abortion. We ring the church bell once for every million babies that have been aborted. Last year we rang it fifty-two times. We want to remind our church members of the tragedy of abortion and renew our commitment to stopping it.

Modern technology has been a friend to those of us who are pro-life. Sonograms can give a very accurate picture of a baby in the womb. They look like the very human beings they are. Leave them undisturbed and they become living, breathing babies. If a baby in the womb is not a human life, what is it?

The very first Christians opposed killing the life in the womb even though the Greek and Roman culture around them practiced it without a second thought. When people become Christians, they become pro-life no matter what culture they grow up in. People who have become Christians in Japan or China become pro-life even though their culture ridicules them. No matter how pro-abortion the media or popular culture is, Christians are still pro-life. I know there are modern churches that call themselves Christian and endorse abortion. They may call themselves churches, but they have ceased to be Christian. Christianity is pro-life.

Another way the sanctity of life shows up in culture is in its value of the next stage of life: childhood. Christianity "invented" childhood, so to speak. Today, we associate children with warm feelings, cuteness, and sweetness, but in the ancient world children meant more mouths to feed and years of waiting for these little humans to become worthwhile contributors to society. The value of children we take for granted today is a result of Christian culture's belief in the sanctity of life at every stage.

Christians cherish their children. In societies where the birth rate is falling, Christians tend to have many more children than their non-Christian counterparts. In fact, we encourage people to have more children: both biological and adopted. In the secular West, families are coming under increasing fire for having more children because of "overpopulation," but Christians are guided by God in deciding the size of their families.

In the world in which Christianity first arrived, children were completely disposable and had no rights. At the father's whim, these children could be killed or sold into slavery. Not so with Jesus Christ. When His disciples were shooing children away, He said, "Let them come to me. For of such is the kingdom of heaven" (Matthew 19:14). Like all other human beings, children are created in the image of God and, as such, possess infinite worth and value.

In the previous section, we looked at the Roman practice of leaving unwanted babies in the elements to freeze or starve. That may have been the cultural norm, but the Christian response was this: Christians would roam the hillsides looking for these abandoned babies. They would take them home and raise them as their own children.

This practice of adoption continued during the Middle Ages. Christians would go to pagan lands and purchase kidnapped children out of slavery. They would then adopt and raise them in Christian institutions.

Adopting children has been central to the meaning of my own life. Early in our marriage, my wife and I felt the Lord leading us to adopt children, and eventually we adopted three. My three adopted sons happened to be of different ethnicity. When we were out in public, we got lots of stares and questions. When people asked me, "Why are you adopting children who are a different race from you?" I would always answer simply, "This is what we Christians do." The word "adoption" is a rich word in a Christian's vocabulary. Every Christian is adopted into God's family (Romans 8:15), so we adopt children into our families. The sanctity of life is part of our lifestyle.

When I was in Cambodia, an orphanage director told me about a Christian nurse he knew. She had gotten word that a family had decided to dispose of their new baby girl. She learned of their intentions and followed them out into the jungle where they put the baby girl in a box and buried her alive. The nurse waited for the family to leave. She then ran and dug up the baby girl. She was perfectly healthy and normal. The nurse took her to a Christian orphanage where believers took care of her. This Christian nurse acted just like the Christians in the days of the Roman Empire two thousand years ago. She protected the life of this infant girl because she believes in the sanctity of life.

Christians believe in caring for the disabled, no matter how disabled they are. A doctor in a Western hospital will ask a pregnant woman if she wants a test to check for birth defects. In most cases where there are abnormalities, the baby's life is terminated. This is not Christian.

I remember meeting with a young woman who had gone as a missionary to a non-Christian country. There she began volunteering in a state-run orphanage. One day a little boy arrived who had Down syndrome and had a hole in his heart. She asked if she could care for him. The orphanage gave her permission to take the little boy home with her to care for him until he died. But he didn't die. Under her loving care, he got better. She asked and received permission to raise money for a heart operation. The operation was a great success, and the little boy was adopted into a Christian home in the United States.

This girl's Christianity saved the boy's life, because she knew that people with Down syndrome have infinite worth and value in the eyes of Almighty God.

Another little girl was brought into the same orphanage. She had been put in a cardboard box and abandoned at a bus stop. A policeman brought her to the orphanage. There, an American teacher and her husband discovered the little girl while volunteering at the orphanage. They took that little girl home, cared for her, and finally adopted her. She is now my granddaughter!

The sanctity of life also applies to the elderly. Christianity has always cared for and cherished the elderly, no matter what their condition. In Western societies that are ceasing to be Christian, the intentional killing of the elderly is becoming more common, often against their will or without their knowledge.

As Christians, we also oppose suicide. Life is a gift from God and you have no right to take it, even if it is your own. Societies in Christian cultures often have laws against suicide. You might ask, "Why on earth have a law against suicide? Isn't it too late?" No. First, it is important for a society to take a stand against the taking of one's life. It is a gesture in law that every life has value. Second, laws against suicide are necessary for the state to intervene in the life of a person who attempts it. They give a society legal room to help a person and try to keep them from trying again.

Cultures that hold to the sanctity of life value every human, at every stage, in every condition.

Conclusion

From birth to death, Christians value life. Our value comes directly from God Himself, not from our utility, our power, our wealth, our success, or any other measure. God is a constant source of worth, and therefore Christians value their own lives. They do not reject God's gift of life in the form of suicide. Because God values others, Christians value others. They protect the lives around them equally, regardless of ethnicity, deformity, gender, or social status. God injected the idea of sanctity of life through a biblical people who stand against every cultural current that had ever existed before. The Bible creates a radically new culture everywhere people obey the Word of God.

CHAPTER 2
The Value of Women

o————————o

Male and female created He them. –*Genesis 1:27*

Since all people are created with inherent worth and value, why are some people so consistently oppressed by others? God's own people, the Jews, have been oppressed and discriminated against in almost every era. Throughout human history, different groups have dominated others, but one group has consistently been oppressed: women. In this way, women represent all those who historically have been put down and overpowered. Only in Christian culture do women have value in the way that God created them: equal to men, but unique from them.

Unfortunately, uninformed people assume quite the opposite about Christian culture. They see the Bible as sexist because the Bible teaches the differences between men and women, especially within the family structure. A young female college student came to me once with a number of verses she had picked from the Bible that she thought were demeaning to women. Before I went verse by verse with her, I asked her this question: "Why are you criticizing the book that has done more good for women than all other books in the history of the human race combined?" This is no overstatement. The spread of Christianity and the growing value of women have been simultaneous.

How does the Holy Spirit of God encourage women to live out their equal value? Well, God does not, as some might wish, empower women to overthrow men and take the power that men have held over them. Rather, the Bible inverts the power structures of this world and reveals the value and power that women, and all the oppressed, have always had in God's Kingdom. When this way of thinking infiltrates a culture, a subtle yet radical revolution takes place: the revolution of Christian culture.

The Biblical Basis for the Value of Women

Biblically, the value of women follows naturally and immediately after the sanctity of life. These ideas are united in the Bible as well. Genesis 1:27 continues on after the portion studied in Chapter 1. "And God created man in his own image; **male and female He created them** [emphasis added]."

This is the most important and culturally influential statement ever made about women. Why? Because both men and women are made equally in the image of God. There is no discrimination in the worth invested in men and women from the time of our creation.

The Bible also teaches that both men and women have equal access to salvation. In the time of the Apostle Paul, certain Jewish religious leaders recited a morning prayer (not found in the Bible) that said: "O Lord, I thank you that I am not a slave, a Gentile, and I am not a woman." In Galations 3:28 the Apostle Paul counters this way of thinking by saying that, in Christ, "There is neither Jew nor Greek, there is neither slave nor free, there is no male and female, for you are all one in Christ Jesus." In other words, all people, regardless of gender, are equal members of God's family.

Acts 16 records a major turning point in world history: the introduction of Christianity into Europe. Who is the first convert on European soil? A woman named Lydia, a dealer in purple cloth.

Jesus is our best example of how to treat each human being with equal value. In John 4 Jesus talked with a Samaritan woman who was sexually promiscuous. She had been married five times and was living with man No. 6. Samaritans were despised by the Jews, women were despised by men, and sinners were despised by the righteous. However, Jesus, the righteous Jewish Rabbi, did not look down on this woman. Instead, he offered her "living water" and the hope of eternal life. He saw her for who she was: a valuable human being created in His image. In Luke 8 we read that Jesus had a number of women who traveled with Him and supported His ministry. He accepted these women as full partners in His mission.

The Bible commands that Jesus' treatment of women be carried out, specifically in the context of marriage. In Ephesians 5 we find the most commonly cited text on marriage. It makes a startling, almost unbelievable comment on behalf of women. Under the influence of the Holy Spirit, Paul instructs husbands: "Love your wife as Christ loved the church" (Ephesians 5:25). This statement singlehandedly elevated the status of wives more than anything written before and was a radical departure from every teaching about marriage up to that time.

The Bible is strikingly different from other ancient documents because it includes the testimony of women. After Jesus was crucified, who were the first to witness His resurrection? A party of women. In Jesus' day, women were not even allowed to testify as witnesses in court, yet here, in the plan of God, they are the first witnesses to the resurrection of the Son of God.

The countercultural inclusion of these women's testimony is no accident. Throughout the Bible, God gives special grace to those who are put down and rejected. In fact, one of the themes of Jesus' teachings is the subverting of earthly power. His most famous sermon, recorded in Matthew 5-7, emphasizes the vast difference between God's kingdom and this world. Matthew 5:5 "Blessed are the meek, for they will inherit the earth" and Matthew 5:10 "Blessed are those who are persecuted because of righteousness, for theirs is the kingdom of heaven," are two verses that reveal who really wins in the Kingdom of God: not the crafty and powerful but the meek and righteous. Women and other oppressed peoples have never been excluded from the kind of power that dominates the kingdom of God. As the Apostle Paul writes later on: "For Christ's sake, I delight in weaknesses, in insults, in hardships, in persecutions, in difficulties. For when I am weak, then I am strong." (II Corinthians 12:10). Jesus himself said to his disciples regarding power,

> "You know that those who are regarded as rulers of the Gentiles lord it over them, and their high officials exercise authority over them. Not so with you. Instead, whoever wants to become great among you must be your servant, and whoever wants to be first must be slave of all. For even the Son of Man did not come to be served, but to serve, and to give his life as a ransom for many" (Mark 10:42-45).

Herein lies the cultural power of the status of women: God values meekness over power, righteousness over dominion, and service over strength. As this truth has spread, earthly power structures have toppled, and the oppressed have been liberated. As Jesus said, "The Spirit of the Lord is on me, because he has anointed me to proclaim good news to the poor. He has sent me to proclaim freedom for the prisoners and recovery of sight for the blind, to set the oppressed free" (Luke 4:18, 19).

How the Value of Women Impacts Culture

Historically, most cultures have preferred men over women. In Christian cultures, women are held as equal in value but different in function. God created two different genders for a reason. While some cultures reject the equal value of men and women, my culture rejects that there even exists a difference between the two. When we reject the differences between the genders, we reject the way God has chosen to reveal his image in humanity. A Biblical culture functions because of the differences between men and women, but it does so without putting down one or the other. Sadly, women in non-Christian cultures are violently oppressed.

The Value of Women in Non-Christian Cultures

I love to ask my students this question: "Do you believe Christians should go around the world trying to change culture?"

The students always say, "Of course not!"

Then I ask them this: "What would you say about a man who went to India and sought to change an ancient religious practice? In fact, he persuaded the British government to pass legislation forbidding the practice. Should he have done this?"

Some students might then ask, "What is the practice?"

"What difference does it make?" I respond. "It's their religion." But then I proceed to tell them what the religious ceremony was.

The Hindus in India practiced "suttee." A widow was required to cast herself on her husband's burning funeral pyre. If she did not do so voluntarily, she was tied to the pyre and burned to death. An old Hindu saying held: "If her husband is happy, she should be happy; if he is sad, she should be sad; and if he is dead, she should also die." After 35 years of effort the missionary William Carey got the practice abolished, but even today it occasionally occurs. However, Christian culture was imposed on India, much to the betterment of women.

Sadly, the mistreatment of women has been common since ancient times. Even respected thinkers were discriminatory, such as the philosophers of ancient Greece. Plato, who lived 350 years before Christ, taught that if a man lived a cowardly life, he would be reincarnated as a woman. If she lived a cowardly life, she would be reincarnated as a bird. Apparently, Plato didn't have a very high view of women. Another one of the famous Greek philosophers, Aristotle, said:

> "But is there anyone thus intended by nature to be a slave …? There is no difficulty in answering this question, on grounds both of reason and of fact. For that some should rule and others be ruled is a thing not only necessary, but expedient; from the hour of their birth, some are marked out for subjection, others for rule. … Again, the male is by nature superior, and the female inferior; and the one rules, and the other is ruled; this

principle, of necessity, extends to all mankind." [10]

So, according to Aristotle, a woman should not even have free will—one of the gifts of God to all humanity. Yet another Greek scholar wrote that a male child was of vital importance, even more than his mother. A male offspring was "her principal source of prestige and validation," whereas a female child was "an economic liability, a social burden." In ancient Greece it was rare for even a wealthy family to raise more than one daughter. This culture preferred males and saw them as more valuable than females.

Many of the practices discussed in the previous chapter singled out women. In ancient Greece and Rome, female babies were far more likely to be abandoned in the wilderness to die. This is why Roman and Greek families were small and had fewer girls than boys. Women have been routinely aborted and/or killed at birth simply because of their sex. In cultures that practiced human sacrifice, most of the victims were women.

When Christians arrived in Asia two hundred years ago, they found female infanticide a common practice. Another famously discriminatory practice was the Chinese "foot-binding," forced on women on a wide scale and practiced up into the 1900s. A young girl's feet would be wrapped to prevent growth, keeping her feet small. The deformity limited her mobility, and must have been terribly painful. This was done because "men like small feet." [11] The preference of men was implemented without the preference of women even being considered.

I wish that the mistreatment of women in our world were a thing of the past, but it is not. A number of years ago I stayed in the home of an orphanage director in Phnom Penh, Cambodia. He related the story of a family that lived just across the street. The mother gave birth to twins. One was a male and one was a female. The family fed the boy and starved the girl. The director's wife went across the street and offered to pay for the food for the girl. At this point the family was willing to feed the baby girl, but until then they were willing to sacrifice the female in order to save the male.

A practice called "female circumcision" is common in Africa to this day. It involves the mutilation of a young woman's sex organs to prevent her from experiencing pleasure in sexual intercourse. The procedure is not only terribly painful, it also leads to many other medical complications.

---

[10] Aristotle, *Politics,* V, 1

[11] M. E. Burton, Notable Women of Modern China (New York: Fleming H. Revell, 1912), 20, 163. Cited in Alvin J. Schmidt. How Christianity Changed the World (Kindle Locations 2629-2630). Zondervan. Kindle Edition.

In some respects, outside Christian culture, discrimination against women is worse than ever in modern day. In her book, "*Unnatural Selection*", Mara Hvistendahl evaluates demographic data worldwide and comes to this tragic conclusion: Around the world today there are 163 million missing girls. In other words, there should be 163 million more girls than there are.[12] What happened? They were terminated through sex-selection abortion and infanticide. One hundred sixty-three million girls. That is more than twenty Holocausts. This is a tragedy of unparalleled proportion and shows how evil and hostile our current age is toward women.

The Value of Women in Christian Culture

Christianity is the only major faith to value women equally. Christianity is also the only major faith in which the majority of adherents are women.[13] In the United States, our big problem is getting men to go to church, because in almost every church service the majority of worshippers are women.

Christ honors and loves women just as much as men. There is no double standard. As Christian culture has spread around the globe, it has brought justice and joy to women. There can be no better news for a woman than that Christianity is spreading in her country. A woman can say, "The representatives of Jesus Christ are here, and my life is going to improve radically." That is not to say that Christianity instantly perfects the treatment of women in culture, or even that each Christian individual treats other women perfectly. However, as soon as Christianity begins to influence a culture, the women in that culture begin to be treated better. In the United States there exists a stereotype of the misogynistic Christian, and some people have had personal experiences that confirm this stereotype. While acknowledging that these experiences are real, we cannot allow ourselves to be blinded to the fact that everywhere Christianity has spread, life has improved for women. Given the option of a culture influence by Islam, for example, there is no contest. Women are honored and treasured in the Christian church throughout the world and through the ages. Women have done every kind of ministry in the church. They have taught, evangelized, started orphanages and schools, spread the gospel, brought healing, practiced works of mercy, and every other conceivable Christian activity.

A great historical example of the Christian value for women is in the an-

---

[12] Hvistendahl, Mara. Unnatural Selection: Choosing Boys over Girls, and the Consequences of a World Full of Men. PublicAffairs, 2012.

[13] See especially David Murrow, *Why Men Hate Going to Church*; David Murrow; Rev Upd. edition (2011-11-01) (1800)

cient Greek and Roman cultures we have already explored. Christian families had more girls, not only because they obviously did not kill their female babies, but also because they rescued the abandoned female babies of other families, thus creating an even higher-than-average number of girls in their families. Christian historian Rodney Stark observed that one reason Christianity grew so spectacularly during the early years of its existence was due simply to the population of Christian girls.[14] When Roman men became of marriageable age, there were too few Roman women to marry. They turned to the Christian community to find wives, often becoming Christians themselves in the process.

Christian marriage is a wonderful institution for women. Five hundred years ago, Martin Luther made what was then a radical observation: that a man's best friend is his wife.[15] Christian culture protects marriage, much to the blessing of women. Her role in marriage is treasured. Christianity demands sexual restraint, and insists on monogamy, partially because unrestrained sexuality and polygamy are so destructive to women. Christianity teaches that women are never to be "kept" or used, but cherished and honored by their husbands. There is no sexual double standard. Women are expected to be morally chaste, but so are men. In the Roman world, women were greatly restrained in their sexual behavior, but not men. In the Christian church, God expects the same behavior from men as He does women (see the chapter on Sexual Ethics). Additionally, Christians promote freedom for women in selecting a husband. Coerced marriage is nearly nonexistent in Christian culture, and the choices of women are honored.

After the Protestant Reformation, female literacy became universal. Why? Christian mothers wanted to be able to read the Bible to their children, and how could Christian fathers disagree? These women did not take the freedom to be educated from men. God changed the hearts of everyone, both men and women, because Christianity promotes education for women just as much as men.

Christians lead the world in opposition to prostitution and human trafficking, institutions that objectify and demean women. When I was in Phnom Penh, Cambodia, I was told that, in that city of one million people, there were seventy-five thousand female prostitutes. Half of these girls were under the age of fifteen. Such a situation would never be tolerated in Christian culture, and Christians fight to restore dignity to women all over the world.

---

[14] This is one of Rodney Stark's arguments in *The Triumph of Christianity*: HarperSanFrancisco; (May 9, 1997)

[15] Taken from "Martin Luther on Marriage"; https://livingbydesign.org/martin-luther-on-marriage/

On a visit to Kathmandu, Nepal, I visited a large evangelical church. A deacon took me on a tour of their facilities. He pointed toward a building and said, "Over there is housing for Hindu widows who have no family. We allow them to live here with dignity." He pointed another direction. "That is a home for young women who were sold into prostitution in Bombay. We go there and preach on the streets, asking these young girls to repent and leave their life of prostitution. We bring them back here, teach them a trade, and allow them to live rich lives." Christianity has transformed these girl's lives contrary to their current culture, because Christianity changes culture from within.

Other modern-day Christian movements include opposition to abortion and infanticide, which indirectly protect large numbers of women since females are by far the most common victims of these evils.

Christianity protects, honors, and values women.

Conclusion

Discrimination is one of the great sins of our world. Christianity elevates women, not by taking over the power structures of men, but by subverting them and giving way to Jesus' kingdom. Christianity has not made modern women more valuable and important. It has recognized that women have always been valuable and important. Christianity empowers women and other oppressed peoples from within, to know their own God-given value despite ill treatment, and to impress their higher value upon the culture around them.

CHAPTER 3
Ministries of Compassion

o———————o

When Jesus saw the crowds He had compassion on them. *–Matthew 9:36*

God has indeed created all men and women in His image, endowing us with value beyond our imagination regardless of gender, ethnicity, or any other circumstance. But what is the proper response of those with more earthly power and resources to those who have less? Should we use our equal value before God as an excuse to ignore suffering? No. In fact, the Bible teaches that God's heart is especially tender toward the poor and needy. When people become Christians, a primary evidence of faith is a deep compassion for poor and sick people.

When I was a little boy, my father hired a poor man to work for him. The man was not especially skilled, but my dad hired him anyway. I worked alongside this man for a few days, and observed his poverty. One night at dinner, I told my dad how poor this man was. My dad said nothing, but the next week I noticed that the man had new shoes. He told me about a generous gift the church—where my dad was a deacon—had given him. As a little boy, I learned a powerful lesson about the compassion of the Christian church. I have learned even more as a historian and pastor.

The Biblical Basis for Compassion Ministries

After God created man in his image in Genesis 1, sin entered the world (Genesis 3). Along with sin came death, and every other form of pain and suffering. What does the Bible teach about the poor, the weak, the suffering? From beginning to end, the Bible teaches that compassion is key to the Christian response to sin and pain. Christians are to help, to restore, and to heal.

The Old Testament Psalms and Proverbs speak to God's heart for the destitute. The virtuous woman of Proverbs is marked by her attitude toward the poor: "She opens her arms to the poor and extends her hands to the needy" (Proverbs 31:20).

Christ's community of compassion has no membership requirements. He had a heart for everyone. Some religious groups boast about their commitment to their own members. That may be laudable in a certain way, but it is not Christian. Christianity welcomes all, no matter what their membership status. A church that does not care for the poor is a church that does not obey God. The Spirit of God states this clearly in Proverbs 14:31: "Whoever oppresses the poor shows contempt for their Maker, but whoever is kind to the needy honors God." God does not love poor people more than rich people, but His heart is uniquely moved by the plight of the poor and suffering. "The Lord is close to the brokenhearted and saves those who are crushed in spirit" (Psalm 34:18). Most people want to get away from poverty and brokenness, but God draws close.

God himself drew physically close to our brokenness in the incarnation of Jesus Christ. While ministering on earth, Jesus cared for the poor and sick. Matthew 14 tells the story of a difficult day in the life of Jesus. His cousin and forerunner to His ministry, John the Baptist, had just been beheaded. Jesus understandably seeks time away with his disciples, but the crowds follow him. What is Jesus' reaction? "When Jesus landed and saw a large crowd, he had compassion on them and healed their sick" (Matthew 14:14).

Jesus Christ defied many social taboos concerning the sick. He did not avoid suffering; he embraced it. For example, Jesus ministered to lepers in a way no one else did. In Jesus' day it was taboo to be around lepers, much less touch them. Yet in Jesus' healing ministry to lepers, He touches them. Jesus also associated with other lowlifes of his society. Tax collectors and sinners were welcome in Jesus' following despite the harm this brought to his reputation. When asked why he tolerated such company, Jesus answered: "It is not the healthy who need a doctor, but the sick. I have not come to call the righteous, but sinners to repentance" (Luke 5:31,32). In other words, only people who realize their sin can be healed by Jesus' compassion.

The culture of Jesus' day, like many in our day, equated suffering and sin. The thinking is this: if people are suffering, then they must somehow deserve it. Jesus thought differently. John 9:1-3 records in this exchange between Jesus and His disciples: "As he went along, he saw a man blind from birth. His disciples asked him, 'Rabbi, who sinned, this man or his parents, that he was born blind?' 'Neither this man nor his parents sinned,' said Jesus, 'but this happened so that the works of God might be displayed in him.' " Jesus' example teaches us to love people who are in need no matter the reason for their sufferings. We do not blame the sufferer for their pain. We try to ease that pain.

But what about the person who has brought his suffering on himself through sinful behavior and bad choices? The blind man obviously did not bring his blindness upon himself, but oftentimes suffering is a direct result of personal sin. A Biblical example of this is King David's adultery with Bathsheba (II Samuel 11). When confronted with his sin, David wrote Psalm 51 as a response, in which he cries out, "Have mercy on me, O God, according to your unfailing love; according to your great compassion blot out my transgressions" (Psalm 51:1). David relied on God's compassion, even in the face of personal sin. However, the Bible never tells us to excuse a person's sin. David suffered terrible consequences for his adultery, even though he received compassion from God. Christians are told to condemn sin, to allow and even to add to the consequences, but we show compassion to sinners. Just like the sinners in Jesus' following, we admit that we are sick people needing a doctor. We show compassion to others because we have received compassion from God.

Our ultimate need for compassion is not to overcome suffering or poverty, but to overcome sin. Compassion ministries certainly provide food and healing, but their goal is not to "end poverty." Their goal is to spread the gospel. Even in the Old Testament, God's compassion was seen as the answer to our sin problem.

"The Lord is compassionate and gracious,
slow to anger, abounding in love.
He will not always accuse,
nor will he harbor his anger forever;
he does not treat us as our sins deserve
or repay us according to our iniquities.
For as high as the heavens are above the earth,
so great is his love for those who fear him;
as far as the east is from the west,
so far has he removed our transgressions from us" (Psalm 103:8-14).

Jesus made the forgiveness of sin possible, and performed the ultimate act compassion by dying on the cross. He did this for us when we were still His enemies. "You see, at just the right time, when we were still powerless, Christ died for the ungodly. Very rarely will anyone die for a righteous person, though for a good person someone might possibly dare to die. But God demonstrates his own love for us in this: While we were still sinners, Christ died for us" (Romans 5:6, 7). That ultimate sacrifice has worked itself through the whole of Christianity, and it is why we are committed to works of compassion.

Jesus' compassion for us not only has mercy on our sin, it also gives us an eternal reward. This is another reason Christians lead the world in ministries of compassion: We sacrifice our lives to serve others because we do not believe this life is all there is. In fact, this life is not very important compared to the next, according to Christian teaching. Without this belief, Christians could not psychologically afford to give up our lives. If this life were all we had, then we would cling to it with all our might. Christians feel no obligation to live for this life alone. In a short time we will all be with the Lord and live with Him forever.

Matthew 25 tells a parable about the end of time. To those who have shown compassion during their lifetime, Jesus says, "Truly I tell you, whatever you did for one of the least of these brothers and sisters of mine, you did for me." This simple story has had cultural power beyond measure. Jesus asserts that if you have ministered to someone who is hungry or thirsty, then you served Jesus Christ Himself. The Lord of glory puts Himself in the place of the poor and suffering and asks His followers to serve Him. And the result? "Come, you who are blessed by my Father; take your inheritance, the kingdom prepared for you since the creation of the world" (Matthew 25:34).

Value for the next life is also the reason that Christians give more to charity than others. Studies on philanthropy show that Christians outgive non-Christians by a large margin.[16] Why? Jesus told us to store up treasure in heaven, not on earth, and we obey Him. Our inheritance in heaven is much greater than any riches we could earn on earth. No wonder Christians are willing to give up their lives in compassion for others, out of service to our Lord Jesus.

How Compassion Ministries Impact Culture

Many people ask: If God exists, why is there so much suffering in the world? Why doesn't He just fix it? The Christian answer to this problem is compassion. To get rid of suffering, God would have to get rid of humanity. Jesus' compassion, revealed to us on the cross, is how God is "fixing" the problem. Rather than getting rid of us, Jesus is changing us from the inside out, and the culture along with us. He is acting out his solution to this very day, through the compassionate ministries of the church throughout the world. The natural human response to suffering is to get away from it. The Christian response is to enter into suffering out of love for the sufferer. This is compassion. It is completely counterintuitive. The pain and sin in this world is so unsettling, people's obvious preference is to avoid it. However, if a culture is to improve, people

---

[16] For a scholarly treatment of this subject see Brooks, Arthur C. *Who Really Cares: the Surprising Truth about Compassionate Conservatism: Americas Charity Divide - Who Gives, Who Doesn't, and Why It Matters.* Basic Books, 2007.

must respond to suffering, not avoid it. Cultural change is sewn in the seeds of compassion.

The Lack of Compassion in Non-Christian Cultures

Without Christianity, cultures are not motivated to help the poor, so they avoid, condemn, or even kill those who are in need of compassion. As people race to get away from pain, they cause more and more of it, resulting in a downward spiral of sin and suffering.

The great Greek philosopher Plato (427–347 B.C.) said that a poor man (usually a slave) who was no longer able to work because of sickness should be left to die.[17] Recall the words of Seneca, the first-century Roman philosopher: "We drown children who at birth are weakly and abnormal."[18] In these ancient cultures, there was no compassion for the weak. Rather than using their influence to help, these powerful thinkers gave in to the notion that suffering should be avoided at all costs. They did not have compassion because they did not know God.

In addition to this, Rome's pagan religions provided no motive for charity. Charity almost always requires a religious motive. Many people in Western culture have no specific religious beliefs, yet practice charity. They do so because they are products of Christian culture and believe deeply in their souls that they ought to give to the needy. These blindly motivated philanthropists ought to seek out the roots of their charitable desire, and trace it back to the heart of God.

A young Christian nurse whom I have known for many years was serving in rural Nepal. Once, as she returned to her rural hospital, her bus stopped near a small village. Everyone got out to see what the holdup was. A young girl had been hit by a vehicle and was lying in the middle of the road with a compound fracture in her leg. This young nurse moved immediately to help her but was stopped. The girl was of a lower caste. She was not to be helped or even touched. The nurse was forced back onto the bus and the little girl was left to die. Without Christ, cultures are without compassion.

There has been a good deal of controversy recently over missionaries who have contracted Ebola while ministering to the suffering. Some wealthy Americans have accused them of being foolish to risk their lives for Ebola victims.

---

[17] Schmidt, Alvin J. *How Christianity Changed the World: Formerly Titled Under the Influence.* Zondervan, 2004. (Kindle Locations 2720-2721). Zondervan. Kindle Edition.
[18] Schmidt, Alvin J. *How Christianity Changed the World: Formerly Titled Under the Influence.* Zondervan, 2004. (Kindle Locations 3261-3262). Zondervan. Kindle Edition.

These people condemn the missionaries, but they do not understand because they do not know Jesus Christ. Christians lay down their lives to help the sick because Jesus did. Where do these wealthy Americans think their wealth and safety came from?

If you travel the world today, you find compassion to be sadly lacking in countries with little Christian influence. Westerners are shocked by the violent disregard for human life. We must remember the philosophical roots of compassion. Entering into the suffering of others is unnatural to human beings. Compassion flows from the heart of God, and is only viewed as reasonable in Christian culture.

Compassion Ministries in Christian Cultures

No historical evidence exists of organized compassion ministries in the world before the coming of Christ. Since Christ's resurrection and the gift of his Holy Spirit, compassion ministries have been at the heart of the spread of Christianity.

Historian Christopher Dawson made this comment about the culture of the early church: "It was this callous, compassionless culture that the Christians entered. Unlike the pagans, they showed compassion in caring for the weak, the sick, the downtrodden, and the dying, often risking their own lives in the process … The Christians in the midst of manifold and malignant pestilences … did not hesitate to devote their services, and too often their lives to the sick." [19]

Tertullian lived in the Roman Empire in about A.D. 200. He informs us that the early Christians had a common fund to which they gave voluntarily, without any compulsion, on a given day of the month, or whenever they wished to contribute. This fund supported widows, the physically disabled, needy orphans, the sick, prisoners incarcerated for their Christian faith, and teachers requiring help; it provided burials for poor people and sometimes funds for the release of slaves. These are causes lauded in the West today, but they were the causes of Christianity alone in that day. [20]

The first ecumenical council of the Christian church at Nicaea in 325 directed bishops to establish a hospice (a hospital) in every city that had a cathedral. In response to this, a woman named Fabiola, a wealthy widow and an associate of St. Jerome, built the first hospital in the West in the city of Rome

---

[19] Schmidt, Alvin J. *How Christianity Changed the World: Formerly Titled Under the Influence.* Zondervan, 2004. (Kindle Locations 2739-2740). Zondervan. Kindle Edition.
[20] Edward Ryan, History of the Effects of Religion on Mankind, 152–53.

in about 390. According to Jerome, Fabiola donated all of her wealth (which was considerable) to construct this hospital. She served at the hospital herself, bringing the sick from off the streets in Rome.[21] By the 500s, almost every monastery had a hospital, and their number was very large. Monasteries had sprung up everywhere and became one of the most common institutions in Europe. These Christian hospitals were the world's first voluntary charitable institutions. There is "no certain evidence," says scholar Alvin Schmidt, "of any medical institution supported by voluntary contributions ... till we come to Christian days." [22] Christianity revolutionized the treatment of the poor, the sick, and the dying.

Compassion ministries continued to spread through the Christians of the Middle Ages: "Every church had its matriculum, or list of persons in receipt of relief, and enormous sums were spent in every kind of charitable work."[23] Entire Catholic orders were built around helping the poor and suffering; for example the Franciscans, or more recently the Sisters of Charity of Mother Teresa. By the 1100s, "some of the religious orders that arose during the Crusades provided hospitals for abandoned and orphaned children. The Order of the Holy Ghost was one such group. By the end of the 13th century, this order operated more than 800 houses for orphans. Many monasteries also cared for orphans during the Middle Ages."[24] By the mid 1500s, 37,000 Benedictine monasteries existed to care for the sick. Historian Will Durant said, "In one aspect the Church was a continent-wide organization for charitable aid."

The Christian Church has been exemplary all through history for its ministries of compassion, and that spirit has continued in Christian charities and hospitals renowned all over the world. Consider just a few examples of recent ministries of compassion:

By the time he died in 1898, George Mueller's orphanages in England housed, cared for, and educated more than 8,000, but it is easy to forget that all this was in service to the least fortunate.

Florence Nightingale (1820–1910), the founder of modern nursing, received much of the inspiration for her work from Jesus Christ.

---

[21] (Letter to Oceanus 5). Schmidt, Alvin J.. How Christianity Changed the World (Kindle Location 3324). Zondervan. Kindle Edition.

[22] Schmidt, Alvin J. *How Christianity Changed the World: Formerly Titled Under the Influence*. Zondervan, 2004. (Kindle Location 3324). Zondervan. Kindle Edition.

[23] Christopher Dawson, Medieval Essays: A Study of Christian Culture (Garden City, N.Y.: Image Books, 1959), 46.

[24] Schmidt, Alvin J. *How Christianity Changed the World: Formerly Titled Under the Influence*. Zondervan, 2004. (Kindle Locations 2794-2795). Zondervan. Kindle Edition.

Prison Fellowship, founded by a convicted felon named Charles Colson, is the greatest force for compassion toward prisoners in the history of the world. When I was a child my church had a "jail service" every Sunday afternoon when men in our church went to the local jail and shared Christ with prisoners. When they came to Christ they came to church. Criminals are not despised in Christianity, because we are all criminals guilty of breaking God's laws.

William Booth, who lived in the 1800s, founded The Salvation Army to provide the poor with inexpensive food. He established an employment exchange to help them find work, founded a missing persons bureau, opened night shelters, a farm colony, soup kitchens, leper colonies, home industries in India, hospitals, schools, and even a lifeboat for the fishermen of Norway—these marked successive stages in the Army's massive program of social action. Permeating it all has been the concern for personal salvation in Christ.

I agree wholeheartedly with Josiah Stamp, the Christian historian who stated: "When modern secularists show compassion today upon seeing or hearing of some human tragedy—for example, massive starvation, earthquake disasters, mass murders—they show that they have unknowingly internalized Christianity's concept of compassion."[25]

The remarkable cultural power of Christianity continues to show itself in ministries of compassion. For example:

"The average human life span in A.D. 33 was 28 years, whereas in 1990 it was 62. While most of that difference comes primarily from advances in the field of medicine, much of it also comes from the widespread boost to health by medical missionaries spanning the globe in the last century or two. Even this very day, tens of thousands of Christian missionaries are providing basic medical services to millions of people in the Third World." [26]

Advances in technology originating in the West spread around the world because of Christian compassion ministries. Historian George Grant records: "As missionaries circled the globe [after Columbus] … they established hospitals. They founded orphanages. They started rescue missions. They built almshouses. They opened soup kitchens. They incorporated charitable societies. They changed laws. They demonstrated love. They lived as if people mattered."[27]

---

[25] Josiah Stamp, *Christianity and Economics* (New York: Macmillan, 1938), 69.

[26] Kennedy, D. James; Newcombe, Jerry. *What if Jesus Had Never Been Born?* (Kindle Location 2650). Thomas Nelson. Kindle Edition.

[27] George Grant. *The Last Crusade: The Untold Story of Christopher Columbus* (Wheaton, Ill.: Crossway Books, 1992), 127.

Of course, this is because people do matter.

I was having dinner with a young man some time ago who is involved in adopting a special-needs child from China. I asked him, "How much will it cost?" He said, "About $40,000." For most people throughout history, this is not a wise investment of so much money, not to mention the time, effort, and pain it will cost the man to raise this child with special needs. But this example is typical of what Christians do.

I was reading a well-known travel guide on India. It said, when you get sick, "Find a Christian hospital."[28] Apparently even this secular travel guide knew that Christianity is the best place to go when you need help.

In 2001 I spoke at a missionary conference in Nepal. I met a number of missionaries. One was not a teacher, a preacher, a church planter, or a medical missionary. He was a farmer, but he was a farmer with a special calling: He wanted to help lepers, just as Jesus did. He bargained with the Nepali government for a plot of land in an undesirable part of the country. He moved there with a colony of lepers and lived with them for a year. During that time he taught them to farm—how to provide for themselves and live life with dignity.

One of my favorite pictures was taken at a rural hospital on my visit to Nepal. It shows a high-caste Brahmin convert to Christianity. He is sitting in a chair, and on his lap is an old man badly disfigured by leprosy. Normally, a higher-caste Hindu would never even touch a leper, much less embrace him. Not only does the high-caste Brahmin have his arms around the old man, but both are smiling—even though the leper has no lips. This high caste Hindu had come to the mission hospital and embraced the Gospel of Jesus Christ. The Gospel transformed the high-caste Brahmin the way it has the whole world.

This is Jesus Christ in action. He takes men and women who would never even touch a leper and transforms us. By embracing us with His gospel, Jesus teaches us to embrace lepers. Christians lead the world in ministries of compassion. We love others because Christ loved us. The world of compassion is the world of God's love, and how we thank Him for His love for all of us.

Conclusion

Suffering and pain are everywhere. Most people avoid these things as much as they possibly can, but everyone experiences the pain of living in a broken world. Some people use suffering as a reason to question the existence

---

[28] Found in the India edition of the well-known series of guide books; this came from Lonely Planet, India.

of God, but this gets them no closer to actually solving the problem. God's answer to the pain and suffering of the world is his compassion. By entering into our pain, our suffering, and even our death, Jesus made a way through the pain of this life. Christians throughout history have followed the example of Christ, and their supernaturally compassionate hearts have changed the world.

CHAPTER 4

Human Rights

○————————○

Let justice roll down like a river. –Amos 5:24

Compassion embodies mercy, but often reality demands justice. Compassion changes behavior from the inside, but justice requires behavior from the outside. Justice does not wait for behavior to change. For example, African Americans have equal rights in America, even though racist Americans still exist. Justice insists on certain behaviors whether people would naturally choose them or not. These determined behaviors, and the consequences for bad behavior, are outlined in laws. Judicial systems uphold the law, and movements of social justice fight for correct laws.

About 100 years ago, before the civil rights movement, my grandfather was a rural pastor in the mountains of Eastern America. He had four different churches that he served, one for each Sunday of the month. I inherited hundreds of his sermon outlines, all of which I have read. A central theme in his preaching was the unity of the human race. People of all ethnicities are the sons and daughters of Adam and Eve, hence, we are all equal. We have equal value, and we are equally under God's law.

Many great intellectuals in the major universities of the world at that time held a different view. They argued that man had evolved from apes. This part of evolutionary theory we are familiar with. However, they held other beliefs we do not reference as part of evolutionary theory anymore. The part of the theory went like this: Some men had evolved further than others. There were several branches on the tree of evolution, and people on the western European branch had evolved the furthest. People on the Asian tree or the African tree had not advanced nearly as much, nor had people from eastern or southern Europe, and neither had the Jews. Therefore, white northern Europeans had evolved into the greatest, smartest, most advanced people in the history of the world. These intellectuals recognized the superiority of Western culture, but they attributed it to evolution and not to Christianity. This view is known as Social Darwinism, which is opposed to social justice. If some people have evolved higher than others, how could the same law and the same rights apply to all?

My grandfather rejected Social Darwinism. He preached against such prejudiced belief. White intellectuals from 100 years ago viewed my grandfather as an ignorant, backcountry preacher. White intellectuals today would say he was right.

True social justice does not find its roots in evolutionary theory. Social justice comes from Christianity. Without a philosophy of equal value, there is no basis for equal rights demanded by law. As my grandfather preached: Since we all have the same parents and are all created in the image of God, we believe that all deserve equal justice under the law.[29]

The Biblical Basis for Social Justice

God established his law through a series of six covenants in scripture. This word *covenant* is key to understanding the way Christians view the law. A covenant is a solemn, binding promise. The primary covenant we understand in Western culture is the covenant of marriage. This is a great example because we know marriage to be a wonderful, desirable institution. We also know that divorce brings heartbreaking consequences. In Judaism and Christianity, obeying God though the law is just like marriage: wonderful, and desirable, a highly motivated personal response to God himself. As David wrote, "Make your face shine on your servant and teach me your decrees."(Psalm 119:135) But, just like divorce, disobeying God's law brings heartbreaking consequences that are deeply personal. Breaking the law is sinning against God himself. Loving God and obeying God are one. Jesus said to his disciples, "If you love me, keep my commands" (John 14:15)

How can God demand our obedience? Because he created reality as it ought to be. His law outlines the behavior he desires as consistent with the reality he created. The law is not a set of rules and punishments God made up. The blessings and punishments in scripture are the inevitable outcomes of acting a certain way. In addition, just like any good parent or teacher, God compounds the natural outcome of our actions with both positive and negative motivation. God punishes sin but blesses righteousness. He demands our obedience for our own good, and because he himself hates sin and loves righteousness.

God makes a covenant with Adam and Eve just after the Fall in Genesis

---

[29] A good discussion of this and related matters can be found in the allaboutscience.org blog. See, for example, https://www.allaboutscience.org/what-is-social-darwinism-faq.htm

3:14-19. In these verses, God lists the consequences for Adam and Eve's sin. Every human since has been born a sinner: a perpetrator of injustice. However, God also promises an end to sin. An offspring of Eve's will crush the head of the serpent, the devil. Injustice will end.

God makes a covenant with Noah after the flood in Genesis 8:20-9:17. God promises relief from his personal wrath and gives the rainbow as a sign. In this covenant, God begins to reveal that he personally will deal with the consequences of injustice.

God makes a covenant with Abraham, the "father of faith," in Genesis 15. Historical studies of ancient covenant making reveal that typically, the lesser party (Abraham) would bear the consequences of a broken covenant, but in this case God himself ceremonially reveals that he will bear the consequences of a broken covenant. In this iteration of the covenant, God reveals his understanding that humanity cannot keep its end of the covenant. In other words, humanity can never be the source or standard of justice. None of us lives up to the good we know through our human conscience, much less the good revealed by the law of God.

God makes a covenant with Israel through Moses, described in detail throughout Exodus, Leviticus, and Deuteronomy. This covenant is generally referred to in the Bible as "the law," because it outlines in detail specific behaviors. The law not only helped the Israelites to live righteous lives and provide atonement for their sins, it also paints a vivid picture through deep symbolism and imagery that is only fully brought to light in the New Testament. The Israelites were living more good than they knew when they obeyed the law. But the law was overwhelming, burdensome, and ultimately impossible to follow as broken, unjust human beings.

God makes a covenant with David in II Samuel 7:4-17. This time, God reiterates the deeply personal nature of the covenant: how the whole world will be blessed by Abraham's family, now more specifically through his descendant David's family. The covenant also reveals the royalty of the promised Messiah, the "offspring" promised to Eve at the beginning of human history. The messiah-king would one day rule in justice over the world.

After David's death, Israel spends generations breaking God's nation, his law, and his heart. During this period of history, God sends prophets to demand justice, the justice forgotten in disobedience to God's law:

> "Learn to do right; seek justice. Defend the oppressed. Take up the cause of the fatherless; plead the case of the widow" (Isaiah 1:17)

"He has shown you, O mortal, what is good. And what does the Lord require of you? To act justly and to love mercy and to walk humbly with your God" (Micah 6:8).

"But let justice roll down like waters, and righteousness like an ever-flowing stream" (Amos 5:24). (American civil rights champion Martin Luther King was fond of quoting this passage.)

The prophets, in the midst of their warnings, continue to look forward to the coming messiah, and the hope of future justice:

"See, a king will reign in righteousness
and rulers will rule with justice.
Each one will be like a shelter from the wind
and a refuge from the storm,
like streams of water in the desert
and the shadow of a great rock in a thirsty land" (Isaiah 32:1, 2).

But the people of Israel ignore the prophets. In consequence, they are taken into captivity. Some hopelessly believe that the covenant is broken beyond repair, but others still look for the promised messiah.

Jesus Christ the messiah brings the New Covenant to earth in his own incarnation, as recorded in the gospel accounts of Matthew, Mark, Luke, and John. Every promise from every iteration of the covenants are fulfilled in his life, death, and resurrection. He is the offspring of Eve, ofr Abraham, and of David. He took on the wrath of God, and the full consequences of the broken covenant. He completely fulfilled the law of Moses. He will reign forever as King of heaven. Jesus' death paid for our lives of injustice and made a way for us to be justified before God.

Now each person on earth has a personal, legal choice: to be justified before God or to stand on his own merit. Our fundamental relationship with God is legal; "it is God who justifies …"(Rom. 8:33) People innately understand this, which is why in all religions there is some attempt to "get right with God" or get the higher power on your side, or get the gods to do what you need them to do. The Christian faith takes care of this notion through Christ's atoning death. His death on the cross satisfies the demand for divine justice.

Jesus said, "For God so loved the world, He gave His only begotten Son, that whoever believes in Him will be saved" (John 3:16). There is no more inclusive statement in any religion. I must agree with Charles Colson that the greatest civil libertarian who ever lived was Jesus Christ.[30] Since his life, death, and resurrection, Christians have brought a great movement of justice throughout the world. Our sin is paid for. We are justified before God. We love the law and do not fear it. We seek justice for others, and for their own justification before God.

God's law reveals that the justice comes from God, that God demands justice, and that he will ultimately end injustice on earth.

How Social Justice Impacts Culture

Social justice is inextricably linked to the sanctity of life, as examined in chapter 1. The reason for this is that equal rights start with equal value. Without the philosophical basis of equal value, equal rights do not have political basis. Equal rights also start with a transcendent lawgiver. If laws originate from humans, then those same humans can change the laws to justify themselves. Under the law of God, no one can justify themselves. We can only be justified through salvation. This also means that the law is a transcendent truth for humans to discover, not a policy for humans to create. Laws are meant to correspond to God's created reality, not to our own personal agendas or politics. Laws should change when they do not correspond to reality, such as the reality of women and minorities deserving the same rights as white males.

Social Injustice in Non-Christian Cultures

The kind of justice, liberty, and rights we assume have seldom existed anywhere else. I have studied the histories of many cultures and, unless they have been influenced by the Bible, they have no human rights tradition comparable to what we hold in the modern world.

Ample evidence of injustice is listed in the other chapters of this book, but here are some additional examples:

In the Greek and Roman worlds, the individual had little value, no rights, and received little justice. He was a small part of the giant state. Other societies of the ancient world never practiced social justice as we use the word today. Neither did they grant individual liberty, individual freedom, fairness before the law, the right to a fair trial, or the right to "life, liberty, and the pursuit of happiness."[31]

---

[30] Cited in Kennedy, D. James; Newcombe, Jerry. What if Jesus Had Never Been Born? (Kindle Location 1423). Thomas Nelson. Kindle Edition.
[31] Thomas Jefferson's famous phrase in the Declaration of Independence.

Ancient rulers subjected their people to arbitrary rule, and did not apply their own laws to themselves. Because they did not recognize God as the source of the law, they unjustly condemned those around them.

We see the same in modern totalitarian states that have departed from the Bible and from the influence of Christian culture.

Malcolm Muggeridge, the great British journalist, was once a non-Christian but later a strong defender of Christianity. He said, "We must not forget that our human rights are derived from the Christian faith. In Christian terms every single human being, whoever he or she may be, sick or well, clever or foolish, beautiful or ugly, every human being is loved by his Creator, who as the Gospels tell us, counted the hairs of his head."

Social Justice in Christian Culture

Where do people enjoy the most political and religious freedom? Which nations have the best human rights records? The answer, of course, is countries influenced by the Bible.

Which countries have the lowest amount of government corruption? I have my students go online and look up Transparency International's country corruption index. Transparency measures the quality of government of every country in the world and ranks them from the least corrupt to the most. The top twenty-five are almost exclusively historically Christian countries, founded on biblical teaching. Transparency is not a Christian organization, nor is it trying to influence the reader in that direction. This is simply the truth of their findings.

Part of social justice is the rule of law. Many historians and cultural analysts think this the greatest contribution Western culture has made to the world: The "rule of law" declares that all human beings are subject to the law; or, the law sits above human whim. Governments are to protect individual rights through enforcement of the law. Governments and their leaders are under the law just as much as private citizens are. Rulers placing themselves under the rules? This only makes sense if the laws come from a higher source than the lawmakers— God himself! Some governments believe they make the laws. Christian governments simply flesh out the laws as evident in God's creation.

The Christian church has been the most committed institution to human rights in history. When Christianity first began to spread, a major catalyst for growth was the Christian commitment to social justice. The great cultural historian, Christopher Dawson, made this observation about the Middle Ages:

"No man was too poor or wretched to be included in this community—even the beggars and the lepers possessed their own spiritual dignity which was solemnly recognized by the powers of the world when the king washed the feet of the poor on Maundy Thursday, and fed them at his own table."[32] The king washed the feet of the poorest member of his society, just as Jesus Christ did.

That commitment has been carried forward into the modern world. When the United Nations charter was written in 1946, it included this statement in its preamble: "Recognition of the inherent dignity and of the equal and inalienable rights of all members of the human family is the foundation of freedom, justice and peace in the world ..." This bold statement comes straight out of the Bible's teaching on social justice and human rights. Without God as the one who justifies, how could human dignity be "inherent" or human rights "inalienable"?

The greatest power of Christian culture is the ability to change people one by one. Social justice in the individual heart produces social justice in the heart of a nation and a civilization.

Conclusion

As Christopher Dawson says, "The only remedy [for injustice] is to be found in that spiritual force by which the humility of God conquers the pride of the evil one." [33] Social justice, specifically human rights, stems from Christian culture alone. Why? Because not only do we believe in equal rights and a transcendent lawgiver, we also have personal motivation for seeking justice because we are personally justified before God. Without the hope of salvation, law becomes burdensome and a temptation. But because of Jesus, we can endure injustice, admit our own injustice, and instead take part in the great movement of social justice that is changing the world.

---

[32] Dawson, Christopher. Formation of Christendom (p. 235). Ignatius Press. Kindle Edition.

[33] Dawson, Christopher. Religion and the Rise of Western Culture (Kindle Location 1900). The Doubleday Religious Publishing Group. Kindle Edition.

CHAPTER 5
Human Choice

○─────────────○

Choose you this day whom you will serve. –Joshua 24:15
"I am the master of my fate,
I am the captain of my soul."
—William Ernest Henley[34]

Throughout all of history, people have asked themselves this question: Do my choices really matter? Am I actually free to make my own choices, or am I predetermined by fate? What am I held responsible for, and what is beyond my control? These are all questions of free will.

When I was a boy there was a popular song on the radio based on the motto "Que Sera Sera." The song goes like this:

"When I was just a little girl,
I asked my mother, what will I be?
Will I be pretty? Will I be rich?
Here's what she said to me,
Que sera, sera, whatever will be will be,
The future's not ours to see,
Que sera, sera."

This cute song about a girl and her mother has a darker implication. The implicit teaching is fatalism: Our choices do not matter. Instead of a personal will, "fate" decides your future. Philosophers pose fatalism as the opposite of free will. Since our choices do not matter, we can live as we want. However, we do not have true freedom because our fate is predetermined. In fatalism, our choices do not matter.

Christianity exists within the tension of human free will and divine sovereignty. Unlike fatalists, we believe our choices do matter. The Christian teaching is that the free will of the individual exists within the sovereignty of God. Our choices do matter, but God's power is not thwarted by our choices. God will

---

[34] William Earnest Henley, "Invictus," accesses 19 July, 2019, https://www.poetryfoundation.org/poems/51642/invictus

accomplish His purposes in the world no matter what, but our choices impact how his purposes are accomplished. In other words, our choices matter and produce a variety of outcomes in our lives and the lives of others, but God is ultimately responsible for the meaning and destiny of the universe. Members of Christian, Western culture believe in free will. We are free to make choices, and our choices change the course of history, and of culture.

The Biblical Basis for Free Will

The Bible teaches that man is made in the image of God as a spiritual being and therefore possesses free will. "Now the Lord is the Spirit, and where the Spirit of the Lord is, there is freedom" (II Corinthians 3:17). God is Lord over everything in the universe, but he has created human beings with the freedom to make choices. Throughout the scripture we see two threads. First, we see the free people of God making choices to follow or not follow God and suffering the consequences. Second, we see the determination of God to deliver his people and reiterate their freedom to choose him.

From the beginning, God gave man the freedom to choose. After God created man, he gave Adam a choice: "And the Lord God commanded the man, 'You are free to eat from any tree in the garden; but you must not eat from the tree of the knowledge of good and evil, for when you eat from it you will certainly die'" (Genesis 2:16, 17). God is clear about the consequences, but he leaves the choice up to Adam.

In every restatement of the covenant, God clarified the punishment for sin, as well as the blessing of obedience (see the chapter on social justice). The book of Leviticus outlines long lists of the results for God's people if they make the choice to obey God corporately.[35]

Throughout the Old Testament, God's people cyclically renew their obedience to God, then fall into disobedience, and suffer the consequences. Slavery, wandering in the desert, and exile all result directly from Israel's disobedience. Their choices caused these results in history.

However, God never forgets his promise to his people. His sovereignty, rather than squelching our freedom, delivers us to a greater place of freedom than we choose for ourselves. The prophet Isaiah, witness to the defeat and exile of God's people, looks forward in hope to the promised salvation:

> "For this is what the *Sovereign* Lord says: 'At first my people went down to Egypt to live; lately, Assyria has oppressed them. And now what do I

---

[35] See especially Leviticus 26.

have here?' … When the Lord returns to Zion, they will see it with their own eyes. Burst into songs of joy together, you ruins of Jerusalem, for the Lord has comforted his people, he has redeemed Jerusalem. The Lord will lay bare his holy arm in the sight of all the nations, and all the ends of the earth will see the salvation of our God" (Isaiah 52:4, 5, 8-10, emphasis added)

In the midst of his people's failure, God reassures his disobedient children that he is their father, and he will take care of them. Even while administering consequences, God reminds his people of the promises he has made, and that he is determined to carry out. He will be victorious, no matter how many times his law is rejected.

When Jesus came to earth, he clarified the central function of man's free will. The most important choice people make is not between right and wrong, but between the true God and false gods. The Old Testament peoples turned to false gods of gold, wood, and stone. The Pharisees of Jesus' day had turned to the god of self-righteousness, while others had turned to gods of pleasure, power, or wealth. No one except Jesus himself completely obeyed the law. Even in the best eras of Israel's history, not a single person succeeded in keeping the whole law. Abraham lied, Moses became proud, and David murdered, but each of these men made the true God the God of their lives.

The Bible teaches that our most important choices are made deep inside our own hearts. In Luke 6:45 Jesus says: "The good person out of the good treasure of his heart produces good, and the evil person out of his evil treasure produces evil, for out of the abundance of the heart his mouth speaks." Will shows itself in action, but not until that will is formed internally. This belief makes the Christian faith operate very differently from other systems of thought.

Author D. James Kennedy wrote about God's commitment to man's free will within his sovereign plan, "The Old Testament tells the story of the fall of man into slavery; God's deliverance of His people; their bondage in Egypt; then God bringing them out after 430 years of slavery. Again, they fell into idolatry in their own land and were taken away by the Babylonians into 70 years of captivity, only to be delivered again. All of this is but mere foreshadowing of the great deliverance and of the great emancipator, Jesus Christ, who came to deliver us from bondage unto freedom."[36] Jesus is determined for his people to be free. He loves freedom, and insists upon the free choice of his followers.

Christianity teaches freedom from oppressive governments and social

---

[36] Kennedy, D. James; Newcombe, Jerry. What if Jesus Had Never Been Born? (Kindle Location 1399). Thomas Nelson. Kindle Edition.

structures, but it emphasizes even more the need to be free from our greatest oppressor: our own sin. Paul writes to the Galatians, "For freedom Christ has set us free; stand firm therefore, and do not submit again to a yoke of slavery" (Galatians 5:1). What slavery is Paul talking about? The slavery of sin. Our sinful patterns work like an addiction, robbing us of our free will and making us slaves to destructive behavior. Our freedom is meant to do good, not harm. As Paul goes on to say, "For you were called to freedom, brothers. Only do not use your freedom as an opportunity for the flesh, but through love serve one another" (Galatians 5:13). Free will is meant for good works, not as an excuse for sin.

Freedom is still only partial on earth. Not only are we subject to human oppression, we are still prone to sin. The ultimate emancipation of God's people is still coming, "the creation itself will be set free from its bondage to corruption and obtain the freedom of the glory of the children of God" (Romans 8:21).

How Free Will Impacts Culture

Cultures are largely based in either freedom or fatalism. In other words, most people think that either their choices do matter, or that they do not. These beliefs about the human will form a culture.

Free Will in Non-Christian Cultures

Most people in the ancient world were fatalistic. The ancient Greek, Roman, and Norse myths all teach that fate is determined by specific entities, and that this fate is inescapable.

Ancient Eastern thought is cyclical, including their depictions of destiny. Reincarnation, infinite cycles, and the "circle of life" mentality can have great benefit when applied to our life on earth. Seasons, holidays, tides, new generations, the patterns of the sun, moon and stars—all these point to a cyclic order in nature (see the chapter on science and technology). However, when applied to our final destiny, this "circle of life" mentality results in a belief system of endless, meaningless repetition with no escape. Astrology is one such belief system. About 1,600 years ago Saint Augustine reasoned that astrology is sinful because to believe that one's fate is predestined in the stars stands in opposition to God's gift of free will.

When cultures deny free will, one result is political oppression. Individuals feel they have no freedom and they rely on authorities to tell them what to do. Democracy cannot exist. One historian observed, "In the modern world command economies deny free will, insisting on controlling the lives of others;

governments often do this. It is slavery by another name—controlling the life of another individual. Being central to [biblical thinking], the doctrine of free will called into question the legitimacy of social structures and customs that limited the individual's ability to choose freely— especially slavery and tyranny." [37]

I was riding with a missionary in Nepal when he informed me of the high pedestrian death rate in that country. He said that villagers believed they only had control of their lives within a 5-foot radius. Outside that it was all karma and beyond their control. As a result, they would wander into traffic, thinking their decisions made no difference.

In Western culture, many people are materialistic atheists. Materialism teaches that choice is a simple matter of brain function. Certain levels of brain chemicals, physical appetites, and neural responses determine choice. This is a form of fatalism. Certainly, all these physical stimuli deeply affect people, but Christianity teaches that free will matters more than our physical limitations. People with unbalanced brain chemicals can choose to take medication. A fasting person can choose to go without food for a limited time. Athletes train their bodies and by choice endure much pain and exertion. Fatalism, even this modern "scientific" form of fatalism, produces the sense of helplessness. People are crushed by their lot in life and do not seek to improve it.

Without the balanced view of man's freedom within God's sovereignty, people are crushed by the weight of destiny, and cultures do not thrive.

Free Will in Christian Cultures

Because Christians believe in free will, they make choices responsibly. Because Christians believe in God's sovereignty, they know their lives have purpose and meaning beyond their own imagination. Unburdened by the need to prove their own worth, Christians can instead pursue good works that fit their own inclinations and gifts. These voluntary acts of will have transformed your world and the whole world. Let's look at four major areas: religiously, politically, economically, and in one of the most powerful ideas in human history: the idea of Progress.

1. Religiously:

In John 4 Jesus talks with a fallen Samaritan woman who has come out to a well to get water. Jesus says to her, "Give me a drink." She was shocked. Jews

---

[37] Stark, Rodney. *How the West Won: the Neglected Story of the Triumph of Modernity.* ISI Books, 2015. (Loc. Kindle Edition, 2299)

hated Samaritans. Then Jesus shocks her more: "I have water that if you drink it you will never be thirsty again." Right then and there Jesus gave her a choice. She could choose to take Him into her life or she could reject Him. She had free will.

Again, humans are created in God's image. One way people are like God is that they can will things. The Bible even leaves eternal destiny in the hands of the individual.[38]

The Christian faith operates upon the free will of each individual. "The Judeo-Christian God is a judge who rewards virtue and punishes sin. This conception of God is incompatible with fatalism. ..."[39]

One example of how free will operates in a culture is voluntary organizations, staffed by people who have chosen the cause of the organization. They have joined because they chose to, not because the government forced them to. Voluntary organizations play a gigantic role in Christian culture. Local churches are the primary example in every age of history. In the Middle Ages, monastic houses sprung up; they were the most powerful institutions in the world for a thousand years and they were made up of volunteers. Independent missions have been the most important voluntary organizations in the modern era and have been the primary agents for the spread of Christianity. "Belief in free will led directly to valuing the right of the individual to freely choose, with the result that medieval Europe rejected slavery— the only culture ever to have done so without external compulsion." [40]

2. Economically:

When I talk to the average American they have no idea how powerfully the biblical doctrine of free will affects economic growth. "If there is a single factor responsible for the rise of the West, it is freedom. Freedom to hope. Freedom to act. Freedom to invest. Freedom to enjoy the fruits of one's dreams as well as one's labor." [41]

Without freedom, creativity cannot exist. As part of our free will, God gave us creative freedom to explore and better our world. The economic growth

---

[38] Joshua 24:15: "Choose you this day whom you will serve."

[39] Stark, Rodney. *How the West Won: The Neglected Story of the Triumph of Modernity.* Wilmington, DE: ISI Books, 2015. Loc. Kindle Ed., 2280

[40] Stark, Rodney. *How the West Won: The Neglected Story of the Triumph of Modernity.* Wilmington, DE: ISI Books, 2015. Kindle Ed., Loc. 2272

[41] Stark, Rodney. *How the West Won: The Neglected Story of the Triumph of Modernity.* Wilmington, DE: ISI Books, 2015. Kindle Ed., Loc. 2657

of our era is stimulated by innovation—the creative power of the human mind. God has given us the ability to use our free will to create new ideas—new ideas in how to do things better.

In the last 300 years, the world has experienced the greatest economic revolution of all time. A person living in America today is 100 times richer than his ancestors living 300 years ago. If you make $10,000 dollars in a year's time your great-great-great grandfather made $100.

There are nearly 6 billion smartphones in the world, but only 20 years ago the only smartphone in the world existed in the mind of a few engineers at IBM. The smartphone had no material existence, but engineers began to take their idea and turn it into a material reality. Companies like Apple took the idea and made it one of the most popular items on the planet. Human beings, given a spirit and the ability to create by almighty God, took an idea and turned it into a wonderful reality. Every manmade material blessing we experience comes into existence exactly the same way. Freedom to create results in innovation, which results in the better wealth and well-being we experience today.

3. Politically:

Free will makes democracy possible because the Christian doctrine of free will teaches responsibility to the wider community. This idea is freedom of conscience: We are to choose the right path no matter what some governing authority might tell us. Spiderman knew, "With great power comes great responsibility." But Spiderman probably did not know that the idea came from Jesus who said, "To whom much is given much will be required" (Luke 12:48). Free citizens sense their responsibility to the wider community. This responsibility comes from the Bible's teaching on free will.

The most dramatic example of this comes from early Christianity. The Christian faith became the only religion in history to rise to prominence in the face of hostility from the dominant culture—in this case the culture and power of Rome. The early believers used their free will to defy the greatest empire the world had ever seen.

4. The Idea of Progress

We spoke above about the sense of helplessness that chained the hearts and lives of ancient people. They believed that life is a cycle one can never escape. But the Bible changed all that. In the Old Testament people had the story of the Garden of Eden but they did not live their lives looking backward to the past like other ancient peoples. God continually renewed his covenant with them, so that they could instead look forward to the future in the coming of the Messiah. It transformed their outlook totally.

The City of God, written in about A.D. 430 by Augustine, took the biblical doctrine of free will and turned it into the idea of Progress. Augustine knew that the people of his day labored under the knowledge that they were deeply sinful, and as a result they had no hope. In *The City of God* he spoke of how people can renew their spiritual energy every day and move forward into a glorious future. Augustine was the most influential historian for a thousand years, and he trained the Western mind to believe in Progress.

The idea of Progress has affected every area of human endeavor. In science and technology, people now believe we can make the world richer and better. We believe in political improvements for all people. In economics we expect growth as if it were the natural state of things. All this has come about because of the biblical teaching that we can change our future by our own decisions. In other words, we can make progress.

This idea affects everything and everyone in human life. "Inventions don't just happen. Someone has to bring them about, and the likelihood that anyone will attempt to do so is influenced by the extent to which they believe that inventions are possible— that is, the extent to which the culture accepts the idea of progress."[42]

Conclusion

Free will motivates humans to dream and to create. The Bible's teaching that men and women are free moral beings is one of the most influential and powerful of all time. Modern ideas like democracy and civil responsibility are dependent upon it. It is yet another idea that has changed the world and emerges exclusively from Bible doctrine.

---

[42] Stark, Rodney. *How the West Won: The Neglected Story of the Triumph of Modernity.* Wilmington, DE: ISI Books, 2015. P.64

CHAPTER 6
Sexual Ethics

○────────────────○

A man shall leave his father and his mother and hold fast to his wife, and the two shall become one flesh'? So they are no longer two but one flesh. What therefore God has joined together, let not man separate. Matthew 19:5,6

As free beings, some of our most important choices are moral ones. The moral expectations of God are listed briefly in the ten commandments (Exodus 20) and expanded throughout the Old Testament. Of all God's moral expectations, however, none has been more crucial to the formation of culture than that of the Christian sexual ethic as found in the Bible.

What is the Biblical sexual ethic? The teaching of the Bible from start to finish is that sex is made by God for monogamous heterosexual marriage. The biblical expectation for both men and women is complete faithfulness before and during marriage.

My daughter encountered a young American who claimed that the Bible does not teach that sexual activity outside marriage is wrong. He argued it is acceptable for a Christian to be involved in sexual relations as long as neither are married. My counsel to my daughter was this: The young man has no interest in Christianity. He is interested in living like an unbeliever. And if he is going to live like an unbeliever he may, in fact, be an unbeliever. This may sound harsh, but the teaching in scripture could not be more clear. Christianity considers sexual purity as evidence of God's presence and power in a person's life, and sexual impurity (including premarital sex, homosexual relations, and extramarital affairs) as evidence that God's presence and power have been rejected.

The Biblical Basis for Sexual Ethics

Christians believe in sexual morality for the same reason we believe in the sanctity of life: the revelation of God Himself. As with every Christian belief, the character of God is the starting point for sexual morality. The Bible declares

God to be a non-sexual being. "So God created man in his own image, in the image of God he created him; male and female he created them" (Genesis 1:27). Both genders display the image of God, but God himself is neither male nor female. He has no gender. God created the world by His will, by His word, not through any sexual behavior. "This was an utterly radical break with all other religions, and it alone changed human history. The gods of virtually all civilizations engaged in sexual relations." In ancient cultures, sexually immoral people were simply imitating the promiscuous sexual relations of their gods. Our God is not a sexual being, but he is the one who designed human sexuality and gave it to humanity as a gift. As the designer, he knows best how sexuality should function.

Exodus 20 clearly defines this specific sexual ethic in the seventh commandment, "Thou shalt not commit adultery" (Exodus 20:14). Some argue this only applies to married people. Not so. It applies to everyone. If you are a young person, God expects you to be faithful to your spouse before you ever meet that person. In the New Testament the Greek word for "immorality" is "porneia." Yes, we get our word pornography from it. In this age of technology, we must include that even virtual immorality is unacceptable to God. Unfaithfulness online is still unfaithfulness.

Jesus upholds these same ethics in Matthew 19, a major passage on marriage and morality. Jesus, quoting the Old Testament, says: "For this reason a man shall leave his father and mother and be joined to his wife, and the two shall become one flesh. So then, they are no longer two but one flesh. Therefore what God has joined together, let not man separate" (Matthew 19:5). Our Lord argues that sexual intercourse is so spiritually important and powerful that it makes a husband and wife "one flesh." This passage also assumes that marriage is a gift to all people, not just for the people of God. Marriage creates a special relationship between a man and a woman no matter what their faith. Sexual ethics benefit all of society.

In fact, Jesus goes even further in His expectations for sexual purity. In Matthew 5:28 he states that even lusting after someone, therefore committing adultery in your heart, is a sin. Our God takes our sexual morality very seriously, specifically in the deep, private sanctuary of our minds and imagination, in our spiritual nature.

If the Bible is so clear, why has sexuality gone so wrong in our world? In Romans 1, the Bible says our descent into immorality begins with a wrong relationship with God. Sexual sin is a replacement for the true worship of God. When men fail to thank God or worship Him (v.21) they then move into every sin, including sexual sin. "For this reason God gave them up to vile passions. For even their women exchanged the natural use for what is against nature. Likewise also the men, leaving the natural use of the woman, burned in their lust for one another, men with men committing what is shameful, and receiving in themselves the penalty of their error which was due" (Romans 1:26, 27). Sexual sin reflects an abandonment of our God.

Sadly, the consequences of this abandonment are dire. I Corinthians 6:9, 10 states, "Do you not know that the unrighteous will not inherit the kingdom of God? Do not be deceived. Neither fornicators, nor idolaters, nor adulterers, nor homosexuals, nor sodomites, nor thieves, nor covetous, nor drunkards, nor revilers, nor extortioners will inherit the kingdom of God." And Hebrews 13:4 affirms that, "Marriage is honorable among all, and the bed undefiled; but fornicators and adulterers God will judge." The Bible is clear that any sexual misconduct is a punishable offence in the eyes of God.

On the other hand, sexual purity honors God. Furthermore, keeping the Biblical sexual ethic reflects the changed life of the Christian, and the influence of the Holy Spirit. I Thessalonians 4:3-5 states, "For this is the will of God, your sanctification: that you should abstain from sexual immorality; that each of you should know how to possess his own vessel in sanctification and honor, not in passion of lust, like the Gentiles who do not know God." (NKJV) In this passage, Paul affirms that sexual purity is clear evidence of God's work in our lives.

Sexuality is so sacred because, just like the Jewish sacrifices of old, sex in marriage has two purposes: One is immediate, but the other is a symbolic foreshadowing of an even greater good than we now experience. This future reality is the marriage union of Christ and the Church. Ephesians states about marriage, "This is a profound mystery—but I am talking about Christ and the church" (Ephesians 5:32). Revelation predicts this future scene, " 'the marriage of the Lamb has come, and his Bride has made herself ready; it was granted her to clothe herself with fine linen, bright and pure'—for the fine linen is the righteous deeds of the saints. And the angel said to me, 'Write this: Blessed are those who are invited to the marriage supper of the Lamb' " (Revelation 19: 7-9). Therefore, when Christians express sexuality in marriage, they reveal to the world one of the clearest pictures of God's love, and our future destiny as the bride of Christ. On the other hand, when Christians express sexuality outside of marriage, they obliterate one of the clearest pictures of God's love

The Bible could not be more clear about Christian sexual morality. When men advocate various forms of sexual immorality, they either not know God, or they are in willful disobedience. Sexual purity is one of the most obvious ways to set oneself apart as a Christian.

How Sexual Ethics Impact Culture

Sexuality is key to culture. Unrestrained sexuality is historically a culturally destructive force. Marriage, on the other hand, is the building block of society. Faithful, loving marriages channel sexuality into a force for good. No other expression of sexuality, no matter how "consensual" or "loving," is obedient to the will of God, or a cultural benefit to society.

Sexual Ethics in Non-Christian Cultures

Unrestrained sexuality is a force of destruction, especially for women and children.

Many people today know that the Greeks were notorious for their homosexual behavior. But often they do not know that Greek homosexual sex was primarily pederasty or pedophilia, that is, an adult man having sex with a young boy who was commonly between 12 and 16 years old.

The Roman Empire has been notorious throughout history for its sexual debauchery: abuse of women and slaves, homosexuality, bestiality, orgiastic rituals, and religious immorality. It was a place where men could engage in sexual relations without restraint, involving young women, slave girls, young boys, and even other men's wives. Archaeologists are astounded to find how overt and public sexual activity was in Romans times.[43]

Non-Christian religions tend to be highly sexualized. The Greeks and Romans exalted public sexual activity in their art and literature.[44] Archaeologists have discovered pottery and frescoes from ancient Rome that give evidence of this. Sex was a public spectacle in the ancient world. Throughout the ancient world and even in many parts of the world today, public displays of sexual activity are the accepted norm. Among the consequences of the unchanneled sex drive is the sexualization of everything—including religion.

In the times of the Old Testament, the nations surrounding Israel practiced unrestrained sexuality abhorred throughout the world today. People expected to find prostitutes in temples. Young women, before they were married,

---

[43] Discussed at length in Alvin Schmidt, *How Christianity Changed the World,* (Grand Rapids, MI: Zondervan, 2004)

[44] Alvin Schmidt, *How Christianity Changed the World* (Grand Rapids, MI: Zondervan, 2004), Kindle Ed. Loc. 1885

were consigned to one of the gods and required to have sex with temple-goers for a year or more. The nations surrounding Israel constantly tempted them to capitulate to this debauchery, even though the prophets of God denounced these evils.

Temple prostitution still exists in our modern world. I spoke with a Christian nurse whom I have known for many years. She specializes in "end-of-life care" and traveled to India to teach seminars on how to improve a person's last days. But sadly, many of the dying people she was trying to help were young women. They had been assigned to a temple, used by the priests, then sold to the general public. When they became too sick with AIDS to serve any longer, they moved into hovels where they lived out the last days of their tragic lives both rejected and forgotten.

One of the great tragedies of our time is sex trafficking—the selling of young boys and girls into a life of sexual slavery. One estimate puts the number of trafficked children at 45 million.[45] The amount of money spent on trafficking is greater than the trade in illicit drugs.

A missionary in northern Thailand was shopping downtown in her city when a local businessman asked her what she was doing in his country. She informed him of her attempts to deliver young girls from trafficking. He said, "Isn't that what they [these girls] are for?" In many places, even today, exploiting young women is considered normal.

In the summer of 2015, I met a missionary in Thailand. One of his colleagues told me that he had rescued more than a thousand children from trafficking. I watched these orphans put on a musical performance, and I was thrilled to watch them sing praises to our God. They had been rescued from slavery and sin, and they were thanking God for the salvation they have in Christ. This story illustrates one purpose of the Christian sexual ethic—to stop the immoral sexual behavior destroying culture.

In the West today, unrestrained sexuality is again destroying culture. Divorce is just as common as marriages that stay intact. Americans expect Christians to celebrate homosexuality instead of condemning it. Certainly, these issues have nuances and demand personal attention and care for divorced and homosexual people. As a pastor, I provide this care. But as a historian I must reiterate: Heterosexual monogamous marriage is the key to culture. Every culture draws a line between acceptable and unacceptable sexual behavior, but no line makes as much sense culturally as the line between married sex and unmarried

---

[45] "Slavery Today" International Justice Mission, accessed 23 July, 2017, https://www.ijm. org/slavery

sex. God created sexuality for marriages that benefit culture.

Sexual Ethics in Christian Cultures

Though our culture does not accept the Biblical sexual ethic now, our society would not exist without it. Dennis Prager writes, "Societies that did not place boundaries around sexuality were stymied in their development. The subsequent dominance of the Western world can largely be attributed to the sexual revolution initiated by Judaism and later carried forward by Christianity. Or, in other words, the sexual revolution introduced by divine revelation from almighty God Himself." [46]

When we Christians look at our world today and see its rejection of sexual morality, we are tempted to give up our beliefs about sexuality. How could the strict sexual ethic apply in the modern world? But let us ask ourselves this question: Did the people of the Roman Empire receive the Christian teaching on sex with enthusiasm? No they did not. The people of that day were more resistant to Christian teaching than the people of our day, who have lived under many Christian influences. Christianity came into the Roman empire with the message that sex outside marriage was sinful and a violation of the will of God. Christians held this view without compromise, and their faithfulness to God set them apart and changed the world. Their example teaches us this: Do not forsake a doctrine of God because people around you hate it. Cultures change, but God does not.

One of the greatest pieces of early Christian literature was about 100 years after the Bible: the Epistle to Diognetus. We do not know who wrote it, but it records early Christian culture taking root in the midst of an unbelieving world. The Christians were reported to "marry, as do all [others]; they beget children; but they do not destroy their offspring. They have a common table, but not a common bed."

In China today, Christians are still known for their sexual ethics. In his book, *Jesus in Beijing*, David Aikman says that so many young women in Chinese higher education are followers of Jesus Christ that women with graduate degrees are stereotyped as Christian. And what is the distinguishing mark of their Christian faith? They practice Christian sexual morality. [47]

Christianity insists that we enjoy intimacy and commitment along with

---

[46] Dennis Prager, "Judaism's Sexual Revolution," http://www.orthodoxytoday.org/articles2/PragerHomosexuality.php

[47] Aikman, David. *Jesus in Beijing: How Christianity Is Transforming China and Changing the Global Balance of Power.* Oxford: Monarch, 2006.

sex. Christianity made sexual relations a private act. The intimate nature of sex that we take for granted does not exist outside the influence of the Bible. Christianity took sexual behavior out of the public eye and put it into the marriage bedroom. American law to this day reflects that Christian influence. Marriage itself was a utilitarian institution in the ancient world, but Christianity exalted it to a place of majesty and glory. Whenever you see the beauty of a marriage in our modern culture, remember Christianity established marriage as the beautiful and vital institution it is today.

Christianity does not tolerate the sexual exploitation of children. In the modern West, even unbelievers who reject the rest of the Christian sexual ethic will agree with this part. They, too, oppose the sexual abuse of children. Every country in the Western world has what is known as an "age of consent" or an age under which sexual relations are forbidden. The age may vary (in the U.S. it is generally 18. In a number of European countries it is 14 or15), but the philosophy is the same: Engaging in sexual relations with children is wrong.

Christianity demands that men and women be faithful to their spouse. This is another Christian value retained among modern Westerners. When I taught at a public university, many couples lived together outside marriage, but even in premarital relationships, people expect each other to be faithful. Unfaithfulness to even a boyfriend or girlfriend is called "cheating." It is not called "exploring your natural freedom" or "just being yourself." Unfaithfulness to a partner was universally condemned by my unbelieving students. This reflects their Christian heritage, even if they do not know it. Contrasted to Roman men, my students are downright religious.

Conclusion

Unrestrained sexuality exploits the weak and helpless. Sexual ethics, rather than stifling this God-designed appetite, create a sacred space for married love. When a culture channels sexuality in the way the Bible describes, children thrive as the treasured fruit of sexual union, not the accidental and unwanted consequence of philandering. Most important, marriage paints a picture of God at work in human life. Marriage builds culture; unmarried sex destroys culture.

CHAPTER 7
Rationality: the Christian Roots of Science and Technology

o——————————o

And let man have dominion over the fish of the sea and over the birds of the heavens and over the livestock and over all the earth and over every creeping thing that creeps on the earth. –Genesis 1:26

No one doubts the world-transforming power of the Scientific Revolution and its brother, the Technological Revolution. However, why have they only occurred in the last 350 years? Civilizations have made technological advances for thousands of years, but only in the last few centuries have these technological advances become the worldwide phenomenon we see today. Together, these revolutions have transformed the world materially more than any other historical event.

My daughter's church recently took several members on a mission trip to Moldova, the poorest country in Europe. They went to run a youth camp for children and teens rescued out of the sex trafficking industry that runs rampant in Moldova. They made this interesting observation: Every one of these desperately poor kids had a smartphone. They hold in their hands a resource beyond the imagination of kings and emperors throughout most of history. The Christian roots of science and technology make these discoveries a benefit, not only to the societies in which they originate, but also to the whole world.

The Biblical Basis for Science and Technology

Biblical theology is the basis for scientific discovery and the resulting technological inventions. Historically, these two theological ideas were the foundation of scientific thought: first, that God transcends nature, and second, that man rules over nature. How are these biblical ideas connected to science? We will take them one at a time.

1. The Transcendence of God

Certain assumptions of Christian theology are necessary for modern science. Even modern scientists who do not believe in God hold certain Christian beliefs about the natural world.[48] The basis for science is this: The natural world is governed by certain fixed, observable laws, called in history "Natural Law." If men can figure out those laws, then they can actually understand and utilize elements in nature. "This conception of the universe as an intelligible order has inspired the whole development of Western science."[49] Nature does not disobey its own laws. For example, an apple seed will grow into an apple tree. This law does not vary. Every apple tree has come from the same kind of seed and not any other. Other laws of nature are gravity, the consistent cycle of days, months and years, and the realities of death and decay, otherwise known as entropy. Without the laws of nature, scientific study could not exist because it could have no basis. If seeds randomly produced different plants, if gravity varied in its force, or if some months the moon did not wax or wane, then there would be no patterns to study. With these laws in existence, the patterns of nature are consistent, and therefore they can be observed, described, and even harnessed in our own technological inventions.

These laws point to an important theological idea: transcendence. If nature consistently obeys the laws of nature, then the laws are above nature. Nature is subordinate to the laws. The existence and power of these laws point to a lawmaker. The creator God of the Bible is just such a lawmaker. Because God governs nature, the laws are worth studying, not only to understand this world, but also to understand the creator God.

Paul made this exact argument to philosophers in Athens. He saw that their gods were not transcendent. In fact, they were barely better than humans in their power and definitely in their morality. He said to the philosophers

---

[48] One of the greatest philosophers of the first half of the twentieth century was Alfred North Whitehead. When lecturing students at Harvard University he raised the question of where science came from. He said "[science arose] from the Medieval insistence on a personal God….[the natural world] was supervised and ordered. The search into nature could only result in the vindication of faith and rationality." Stark, Rodney. *The Victory of Reason: How Christianity Led to Freedom, Capitalism, and Western Success.* New York: Random House Trade Paperbacks, 2006.

[49] Dawson, Christopher. *The Formation of Christendom.* San Francisco: Ignatius Press, 2008. P.35

in Athens,

> "The God who made the world and everything in it is the Lord of heaven and earth and does not live in temples built by human hands. And he is not served by human hands, as if he needed anything. Rather, he himself gives everyone life and breath and everything else. From one man he made all the nations, that they should inhabit the whole earth; and he marked out their appointed times in history and the boundaries of their lands. God did this so that they would seek him and perhaps reach out for him and find him, though he is not far from any one of us. 'For in him we live and move and have our being.'" (Acts 17:24-28)

In this simple argument, Paul explains a deep theological truth: God is above nature. In other words, God is transcendent. He governs nature. He does not live in a temple, or on an earthly mountain like the Greek gods did. Moreover, God's plan is for men to seek Him. God's transcendence above nature begs men to study and discover Him in His creation.

In a future letter, Paul makes this statement about how God makes himself known to people through nature: "What may be known about God is plain to them, because God has made it plain to them. For since the creation of the world God's invisible qualities—his eternal power and divine nature—have been clearly seen, being understood from what has been made, so that people are without excuse." (Romans 1:20) According to this passage, nature and its laws clearly direct everyone to a transcendent God.

Without the order of natural law, studying nature would be worthless, and science impossible. Natural law makes science possible. The revelation of God through natural law makes science irresistible to those who seek God. Thus, science arose through the Christian motivation to discover God's qualities in what He has made.

2. The Dominion of Man

Humanity is not transcendent like God. We are part of nature rather than separate from it, like God is. However, our transcendent God ordained that humanity rule over nature. A passage in Genesis continues the passage studied throughout this whole book: "So God created mankind in his own image, in the image of God he created them; male and female he created them. God blessed them and said to them, 'Be fruitful and increase in number; fill the earth and subdue it. Rule over the fish in the sea and the birds in the sky and over every living creature that moves on the ground'" (Genesis 1:27, 28). In this passage, God gave the natural order to man to tend and govern.

Part of man's dominion over nature includes study. Because God is transcendent, humanity may not recognize him unless they are seeking Him. Looking again at Paul's argument in Athens, "God did this so that they would seek him and perhaps reach out for him and find him, though he is not far from any one of us" (Acts 17:27, 28). The dominion of man puts the ball in the human court, so to speak. God filled nature with evidence of Himself, but humanity is responsible to find that evidence and give glory to God. The laws of nature are so orderly and consistent, that men can discover them through observation and simple testing. God has the power to change the laws of nature on a whim, but his purpose is for men to find him. He never acts on a whim. His nature is an orderly argument for his existence as creator. God has also given humanity the freedom to harness and utilize the natural elements and laws to form inventions and technologies. The responsibility and power of dominion over nature shows God's love for man and His desire to work in tandem with humanity to accomplish His purposes in the world.

Historian Christopher Dawson points out that, "It is only in recent times that men like A.N. Whitehead have recognized that modern science itself could hardly have come into existence had not the Western mind been prepared by centuries of intellectual discipline to accept the rationality of the universe and the power of the human intelligence to investigate the order of nature."[50] Coupled with God's transcendence, the dominion of man unlocks the doors of science and technology like no other ideas in history. A critic might argue that Christianity did not play a dominant role in the rise of science but then the critic must answer this question: Why did science and technology arise in Christian culture and only in Christian culture? Was that just a coincidence or is there a causal relationship? The historical evidence points to Christianity as the source of science and technology.

How Science and Technology Impact Culture

Science and technology benefit culture enormously, but they also bring about quick and sometimes startling change. If a culture accepts innovation and change, then science and technology can be implemented. If a culture encourages innovation and progress, then science and technology will thrive and become even more influential. On the other hand, if a culture fears or rejects innovation and change, then science and technology are not welcome.

---

[50] Ibid., p.36

Science and Technology in Non-Christian Cultures

Before the scientific revolution, the world was a place of ignorance and poverty. It was a world that believed individual and random spirits lived in animals and plants, so they could not be studied scientifically. They had no pattern and obeyed no law. Material suffering was the common lot of mankind. William Rosen, a historian of technology, gives this sobering account:

> "By any quantifiable measure, including lifespan, calories consumed, or child mortality, the lived experience of virtually all of humanity didn't change much for thousands of years after the Agricultural Revolution spread around the globe. Aztec peasants, Babylonian shepherds, Athenian stonemasons, and Carolingian merchants spoke different languages, wore different clothing, and prayed to different deities, but they all ate the same amount of food, lived the same number of years, traveled no farther—or faster—from their homes, and buried just as many of their children." [51]

Although Muslim culture developed some science, "Islam holds that the universe is inherently irrational— that there is no cause and effect—because everything happens as the direct result of Allah's will at that particular time. Anything is possible. Attempts at science, then, are not only foolish but also blasphemous, in that they imply limits to Allah's power and authority." [52] Muslim thought holds to the transcendence of Allah, but not to the dominion of man.

In Chinese culture, empires and kings often opposed scientific research. "The reason so many innovations and inventions were abandoned or even outlawed in China had to do with Confucian opposition to change on grounds that the past was greatly superior. Many inventions come from Chinese culture, but no revolution took place because the culture opposed change." [53] China stifled its own technologies and rarely shared them with the rest of the word.

The cultures of the ancient world were hostile to invention and the most crucial ingredient of technological change is that a culture is open to it. Christian culture not only supports change, but believes that God gave humanity power and responsibility to bring that change. The love for innovation we have in American culture today comes directly from Christianity.

---

[51] Rosen, William. The Most Powerful Idea in the World: A Story of Steam, Industry, and Invention (Kindle Locations 110-111). Random House, Inc.. Kindle Edition.
[52] Reilly, Robert R. The Closing of the Muslim Mind. Wilmington: ISI Books
[53] Stark, Rodney. *How the West Won: The Neglected Story of the Triumph of Modernity.* Wilmington, DE: ISI Books, 2015.

Science and Technology in Christian Cultures

The ideas of God's transcendence and man's dominion took many centuries to penetrate the minds of people. The first great scientific advances were made in Western Europe during the Middle Ages (A.D. 1000-1350), and by the end of this era Europe was the most scientifically and technologically advanced culture in the history of the world. For example, in the 1200s, spectacles and the mechanical clock were invented. These inventions, among others, are what historian James Hannam states "catapulted medieval Europe into first place in the race to become the most technologically advanced civilization on earth. Although he did not know it, medieval man had already surpassed China, Islam, and the ancient world."[54]

During this period, the Europeans were making strides so enormous they themselves did not realize how great their gains were. "Europe had long been ahead of the rest of the world in technology, but by the end of the 16th century that gap had become a chasm."[55]

How did this happen? Intelligence was present all over the world. Muslim and Chinese inventions may have been more advanced, but they were lacking the key ingredient: culture. Christopher Dawson explains the necessity of cultural acceptance for innovation:

"While it is impossible to deny the reality of individual genius and the creative achievement of individuals, this is only one side of the story. A genius is also the member of a society, the bearer of a culture and a link in a tradition. Unless the conditions of his culture are favorable, the genius cannot do his work, and even if he did, his discovery would be sterile" [56]

The point Dawson makes here is that inventions themselves are not enough. A whole culture must be open to implementing new technologies before they actually produce lasting change. It took Christian culture shaped by the Bible to produce the scientific and technological revolutions.

A culture becomes accepting of scientific advances, partially by means of education. By about A.D. 1000, great thinkers in the Western world began to ask questions about the natural world. The rational study of God and his creation is the root of modern education. Christians believe that dominion is given to all humans, and that everyone made in the image of God is rational

---

[54] Hannam, James. The Genesis of Science: How the Christian Middle Ages Launched the Scientific Revolution (p. 146). Regnery Publishing. Kindle Edition.
[55] Rodney Stark, How the West Won, Location 3390, Kindle Edition.
[56] Dawson, Christopher. Formation of Christendom (p. 61). Ignatius Press. Kindle Edition.

like He is. The logical result is an emphasis on education. Due to these Christian ideas, Western culture has led the way in universal education, the formation of universities, the education of women, and the education of all classes of people down to the very poorest citizens.

One of the greatest groups of scholars during the middle ages were called the Scholastics. "They founded Europe's great universities, the first universities in history. They formulated and taught the experimental method, and launched Western science. These new institutions distinguished themselves by not limiting their scholarly work to reciting the received wisdom. Instead, the Scholastics who founded universities esteemed innovation"[57] This prized innovative spirit launched the scientific revolution.

Education and rationality continued to spread during the reformation, this time through the promotion of literacy. Christians believe that God communicates with man in written form through the Bible. Therefore, it is of greatest importance that men and women be able to read. In his book on India, *In Spite of the Gods*, Edward Luce bemoans the fact that so many Indians are still illiterate—more than half a billion. And then Luce makes an interesting comment. He says it is too bad that India "has never had a Martin Luther."[58] Luce is referring to the great Protestant reformer who lived in Germany in the 1500s. Luther led the way in education for all, and was determined for everyone to have a Bible in their own language.

Education promoted rationality, and furthered the scientific revolution by informing all of their own God-given abilities to think, understand, and innovate. More educated people meant more scientists and inventors, but it also resulted in a culture of people who believed in the rationality of God, and of their own minds. The West had the key ingredient: culture.

Today, we experience a world vastly changed because of technology, but our advances include some complicated realities. More technology gives humans more power, which can lead to many ethical dilemmas. You will hear many people decry the modern technological revolution, warning about harmful side effects and dangers. However, notice that no one ever declines the blessings of technology. In fact, no society has ever turned down all the blessings of technology. Some groups will forgo certain technologies, but without fail they will keep others.

I laugh at my students who say they want to go camping "to get away from

---

[57] Rodney Stark, How the West Won, Location 3061, Kindle Edition.
[58] Luce, Edward. *In Spite of the Gods: The Rise of Modern India.* New York: Anchor Books, 2012. p.324

it all." In "getting away from it all" they wear synthetic clothing (Gore-Tex for example is a synthetic material that repels water but still allows the fabric to breathe); they eat freeze-dried food; they use a camp stove that runs on white gas or propane; they have pills or filters to purify their water. In other words, they take along every advantage technology offers. And if they get sick or injured they can even depend on a helicopter rescuing them and saving their life. So much for "getting away from it all."

These examples illustrate that the blessings of technology far outweigh the problems. Today, we are awash in a sea of material blessings our ancestors could not even dream of. Instead of complaining about the complications of technology, let us consider some of its blessings.

Transportation

Every summer I load my pickup truck and head for Canada to go fishing. I drive about 1,400 miles on pavement, then 90 miles on gravel, then four miles on a trail cut through the wilderness. I then put all my gear in a boat and travel by water another two miles to my cabin. There I enjoy the spectacular beauty of the Canadian wilderness and some of the very best fishing in the world. By the standards of my country, I am not a rich man. But the richest man in my country would have had great difficulty doing this 100 years ago. My great-grandfather never traveled even 20 miles from his birthplace. The scientific revolution in transportation has given me opportunities the very rich did not have even a few decades ago.

Health

In 1861, Queen Victoria's husband, Prince Albert, died of typhoid fever. The Prince was 42 and one of the richest and most powerful men in the world. He died of something that does not kill even the poorest of Americans today, because it has been eradicated through the science of inoculation. What killed the very rich 150 years ago does not bother the poorest of our citizens today because of the improvements in medical technology.

In the last 100 years, the increase in life expectancy has been remarkable all over the world. I have spent a good deal of time visiting missionaries in Cambodia. Life expectancy in that country is 65, one of the lowest in the world. The life expectancy in the United States in the year 1900 was 47. An American living in New York City in 1900 would not be expected to live as long as a Cambodian villager today.[59] All this is due to the application of technology to health.

Food

Today, the world produces more food per person than at any other time in history. Yes, there is still hunger in the world—far too much, but the problem is distribution, not production. We have enough food. The problem is getting it to the right people. Ironically, in America, the biggest nutrition problem of poor children is obesity. The fact that we produce so much food is a modern miracle of technology. This technology was developed by a simple farmer. He is one of the greatest people you have never heard of: Norman Borlaug. He was born on a farm in Iowa in 1914 and attended the University of Minnesota. He devoted his entire life to improving food crops and was especially successful with wheat and rice. Known as the father of the "Green Revolution," the application of technology to agriculture, he is credited with saving more than a billion people from starvation.

Communication and Computer Science

No technology has created more change than the invention of the smartphone. Not only can it connect people in virtually any location, it puts a computer in your pocket that is more powerful than any possessed by the U.S. government 75 years ago. In fact, the first computer weighed 50 tons. Your smartphone weighs a few ounces and has 25,000 times more memory than that government computer. It is a marvel of technology and brings people endless blessings.

Consider these innovations and more, and give glory to God. He is the one who made the universe rational, and invited human beings study and invent.

Conclusion

Modern science and technology are motivated by these ideas: that God's natural laws exist, and that He has given men dominion over nature. The scientific and technological revolutions that swept our world are not just a matter of invention. The members of Western culture that accepted and implement-

---

[59] In 1900 the life expectancy of an average American was 47; https://www.seniorliving. org/history/1900-2000-changes-life-expectancy-united-states/
Today, the life expectancy of a Cambodian villager is 65; https://www.cia.gov/library/pub- lications/the-world-factbook/rankorder/2102rank.html

ed these progressive ideas and technologies are also responsible for the better world we have today. Together, Christian theology and these people have created a culture of progress and innovation that has blessed the whole world.

CHAPTER 8
More Christian Ideas that Changed the World

o————————o

Every good gift and every perfect gift is from above, and comes down from the Father.
–James 1:17

We have covered seven key cultural ideas that have changed the world. These ideas are found in the Bible and only in the Bible. They are the most powerful ideas shaping culture that have ever existed.

However, there are a number of other cultural values that Christianity greatly encourages. These are positive values that help a culture greatly.

Labor is Sacred

Many cultures place a high value on labor, but others do not. Some encourage hard work, and some see hard work as appropriate for only the lower members of society. Christian culture puts a premium on hard work and discipline. Jesus Christ Himself devoted the bulk of His life to hard work. In His day, a carpenter was a skilled craftsman, but the work was also very challenging physically. The Bible shows its commitment to work by revealing that the Son of God Himself knew how to work hard.

The biblical work ethic begins in the first book of the Bible. In Genesis 2:15 we find that God, shortly after creating Adam, put him in the garden of Eden "to work it and keep it." Dozens of passages in the Bible encourage diligence in physical labor. For example, Proverbs 12:11: "Whoever works his land will have plenty of bread." Solomon also gives this warning in Proverbs 18:9, "Whoever is slack in his work is a brother to him who destroys." In the New Testament, the Apostle Paul tells the church, "If anyone is not willing to work, let him not eat." (II Thessalonians 3:10)

In the Roman Empire work was considered the task of slaves. "Notions of the dignity of labor were incomprehensible in ancient Rome or any other pre-capitalist society." [60] However, Christianity radically changed the way the world views work. It became clear in the Middle Ages that "The true end of labor was not … profit, but the service of others."[61] The ideal for craftsmen was no less high. Historian Christopher Dawson cites this view from a medieval writer: "It is good and true work when craftsmen by the skill and cunning of their hands in beautiful buildings and sculptures spread the glory of God, and make men gentle in their spirits, so that they find delight in all beautiful things, and look reverently on all art and handicraft, as a gift of God for the use, enjoyment and edification of mankind."[62]

A high view of labor encourages human health, study, and progress. From the beginning, Christian culture has placed the highest value on labor. What a blessing this has been to its own citizens and to the world!

Education

Christians believe that one of the primary ways God communicates with man is in written form through the Bible. Therefore, it is of greatest importance that men and women be able to read. The logical result is an emphasis on education. Western culture has led the way in universal education, the formation of universities, the education of women, and the education of all classes of people down to the very poorest citizens.

We cited this quote by Edward Luce in an earlier chapter: Luce bemoans the fact that so many Indians are still illiterate—more than half a billion. He then comments that it is too bad that India "has never had a Martin Luther." Luce is referring to the great Protestant reformer who lived in Germany in the 1500s. Luther led the way in education for all, and was determined for everyone to have a Bible in their own language. India was missing this and suffered for it.

Christian culture created universities. The first were begun in Europe in the 1200s. "Culture is carried primarily in the mind through ideas; the great universities were developed because of the importance of the life of the mind."

Christian culture has dominated education from the beginning and continues to do so. It is a wonderful gift to the world community.

---

[60] Stark, Rodney. *How the West Won: The Neglected Story of the Triumph of Modernity.* Wilmington, DE: ISI Books, 2015.
[61] Dawson, Christopher. *The Formation of Christendom.* San Francisco: Ignatius Press, 2008. P.237
[62] Ibid., p.238

Separation of Religion and Government

Christianity is not generally a revolutionary force politically because religiously it lives in two realms—the religious and the social/political. The Christian faith feels no obligation to overthrow the latter. Christianity is the only religion like this. All other religions combine their religious authority with some sort of control of government. Christianity promotes freedom of religion because of its emphasis on free will. Christians can only truly accept salvation by choice.

Missionary Zeal

Christianity has been by far the most aggressive missionary-minded religion. "For what distinguishes Western culture from the other world civilizations is its missionary character—its transmission from one people to another in a continuous series of spiritual movements."[63] Not only does it spread its message of salvation but it is also committed to spreading an entire culture—religion, education, social values, science, and all other elements of culture. Christianity spreads by influence, not force. Once, a student came to my home and began to complain about "all those forced Christian conversions." I told her, "There has never been a successful forced conversion in the history of the Christian faith. People may have feigned being forced to convert but those conversions are never real, nor are they desirable. Conversion to Christianity must be voluntary to be true."

This has led, among other results, to vast exploratory expeditions. For example, the Franciscans at the end of the Middle Ages explored much territory, and "the journeys of the Friars, no less than the voyages of Columbus and Vasco da Gama, mark the awakening of a European world consciousness and the end of the geographical Dark Ages."[64] The father of the modern Age of Discovery, Prince Henry of Portugal, was a devout Christian who wanted to reach the entire world with the Christian Gospel. David Livingstone is the greatest European explorer in the history of Africa. He was the most famous member of the Royal Geographical Society and a pioneer in that field. Sadly, it is easy to forget is that he was first and foremost a missionary who had a passion to reach the tribes of Africa with the Gospel of Christ (A project that has finally come to fruition in the last 60 years).

These ideas, shared by some other cultures, are promoted to their high-

---

[63] Dawson, Christopher. *Religion and the Rise of Western Culture.* New York: Doubleday, 1991. Kindle edition, Loc. 201
[64] Ibid., loc. 3357

est level by the Christian faith. And they are also ideas that have changed the world.

Conclusion

Seven Ideas Have Changed the World But How Do I Change My Own Life?

In 1953 Sir Edmund Hillary and the Nepali Sherpa, Tenzing Norgay, did what no one thought possible—they climbed to the summit of Mt Everest, the highest mountain in the world, and breathed the thin air of 29,000 feet (8,840 meters) in elevation.

The reader of this book has just done this in the history of ideas. You have reached the summit of human thought, the greatest and highest ideas in the history of the human race.

These ideas have blessed your life and the lives of the people you love but there is another step to take. Jesus Christ has the power to transform tribes, nations, and civilizations so it stands to reason that He can transform your life. You do not have to be the person you are now. The Bible teaches that if anyone is in Christ they are a "New Creation." You can be come a brand new person right now and have your own personal "civilization" transformed.

Admit that you need help and then ask Jesus to do three things. First, ask Him to forgive you for your sins. This is why He died on the cross—to take your place and pay the penalty for your sins. Second, ask Him to come into your heart and take over your life. Let Him have control. Third, ask Him what you should do with your life. Very soon He will begin to open new paths for you—paths of love, power, and peace.

In 65 A.D. the traveling missionary, Paul, wrote to the Roman people. They were citizens of the most powerful empire that had ever been known. He told them, "If you confess with your mouth that Jesus is Lord, and believe that God has raised Him from the dead, you will be saved." (Romans 10:9) That can be your life right now. A new life raised from your old dead life and dedicated to the service of Christ. And Jesus will transform you the same way He has the great civilizations you read about above.

You have read about ideas that have changed the world. Now you have an idea of how to change your own life.

Bibliography

Aikman, David. *Jesus in Beijing: How Christianity Is Transforming China and Changing the Global Balance of Power.* Monarch, 2006.

Aristotle, and H. Rackham. *Aristotle: Politics.* Heinemann, 1959.

Brooks, Arthur C. *Who Really Cares: the Surprising Truth about Compassionate Conservatism: Americas Charity Divide - Who Gives, Who Doesn't, and Why It Matters.* Basic Books, 2007.

Burton, Margaret E. B. 1885. *Notable Women of Modern China.* Nabu Press, 2010.

Central Intelligence Agency, Central Intelligence Agency, 1 Feb. 2018, https://www.cia.gov/library/publications/the-world-factbook/.

Dawson, Christopher. *The Formation of Christendom.* Sheed and Ward, 1967.

Dawson, Christopher. *Medieval Essays, By Christopher Dawson.* 1968.

Dawson, Christopher. *Religion and the Rise of Western Culture.* Doubleday, 1991.

Hannam, James. *The Genesis of Science: How the Christian Middle Ages Launched the Scientific Revolution.* Regnery Pub., 2011.

Hvistendahl, Mara. *Unnatural Selection: Choosing Boys over Girls, and the Consequences of a World Full of Men.* PublicAffairs, 2012.

Kennedy, D. James, and Jerry Newcombe. *What If Jesus Had Never Been Born?: the Positive Impact of Christianity in History.* T. Nelson Publishers, 2001.

Lamb, Harold. *Hannibal: One Man against Rome.* Doubleday, 1985.

Luce, Edward. *In Spite of the Gods: the Rise of Modern India.* Anchor Books, 2012.

"Martin Luther on Marriage: 7 Quotes in 7 Days." *Living by Design Ministries,* 4 Feb. 2018, https://livingbydesign.org/martin-luther-on-marriage/.

Murrow, David. *Why Men Hate Going to Church.* Thomas Nelson, 2011.

Patel, Rita. *May You Be the Mother of a Hundred Sons: the Practice of Sex Selective Abortion in India.* The University Center for International Studies, The University of North Carolina at Chapel Hill, 1996.

Person. "Dennis Prager -- Judaism's Sexual Revolution_ Why Judaism (and Then Christianity) Rejected Homosexuality - Instruction Manuals - The Best Way to Share & Discover Documents." *DocGo.Net,* DocGo, 25 July 2017, https://docgo.

net/dennis-prager-judaism-s-sexual-revolution-why-judaism-and-then-christianity-rejected-homosexuality.

Prescott, William Hickling. *History of the Conquest of Mexico: with a Preliminary View of the Ancient Mexican Civilization and the Life of the Conqueror Hernando Cortés.* Folio Society, 1994.

Reilly, Robert R. *The Closing of the Muslim Mind: How Intellectual Suicide Created the Modern Islamist Crisis.* ISI Books, 2015.

Rosen, William. *The Most Powerful Idea in the World: a Story of Steam, Industry, and Invention.* University of Chicago Press, 2012.

Ryan, Edward. *The History of the Effects of Religion on Mankind ; in Countries, Ancient and Modern, Barbarous and Civilized ... by ... Edward Ryan.* Printed for J.F. and C. Rivington, 1788.

Schmidt, Alvin J. *How Christianity Changed the World.* Zondervan, 2004.

Slavery Today | International Justice Mission. https://www.ijm.org/slavery/.

Stamp, Josiah Lord, and Rufus M. Jones. *Christianity and Economics.* Macmillan, 1939.

Stark, Rodney. *The Triumph of Christianity: How the Jesus Movement Became the Worlds Largest Religion.* HarperOne, 2011.

Stark, Rodney. *How the West Won: the Neglected Story of the Triumph of Modernity.* ISI Books, 2015.

Stark, Rodney. *How the West Won: the Neglected Story of the Triumph of Modernity.* ISI Books, 2015.

Acknowledgments

○────────────────○

This book was inspired by my time with the Akha Foundation in northern Thailand. The director, Aje Kukaewkasem challenged me to write a book on a lecture I gave on how the Bible transforms culture. The Akha tribal group has only had a written language since the 1950s and are showing a significant response to the Christian message. This book is designed for them and other new generations of Christians how the Bible will shape and transform their culture.

Much thanks to my editor, Hannah Pearman, for many helpful comments and insights. Thanks also to Mike Judson of the Denver Post for proofreading the final draft and making helpful changes. Much appreciation is due the Beecher Island Sunday School for listening patiently as the first drafts of this book were read to them. I am grateful to my students at Colorado Christian University for their feedback on many of these ideas, and as always, much thanks to my wonderful helpmeet, Nancy, whose constant encouragement has helped me finish this book.

CPSIA information can be obtained
at www.ICGtesting.com
Printed in the USA
FSHW021959090821
83949FS

9 781734 239003